Improving Pupil Motivation Together

Improving Pupil Motivation Together provides a refreshing and much-needed focus on how motivation can be enhanced by teachers and teaching assistants working both individually and collaboratively. Written in an accessible and engaging manner, the book explores various theories of motivation from a range of perspectives, applying academic theory to real life classroom situations. Using a combination of case studies and empirical research, this book demonstrates how teachers and TAs can successfully enhance the motivation of their students through collaborative practice. *Improving Pupil Motivation Together* starts by introducing theories of learning and motivation and goes on to offer insight in areas including:

- Collaboration and ways to collaborate
- Motivation and giftedness
- Assessment for learning
- Learning goals and learning objectives
- Common pupil responses
- Research in action.

Improving Pupil Motivation Together is an ideal resource for both teachers and teaching assistants working with pupils who are difficult to motivate and who find learning challenging. This book will also be highly useful for teachers managing their support staff and for trainee teachers looking to develop their skills in motivating and engaging pupils.

Susan Bentham is a Senior Lecturer in the School of Education at the University of Chichester.

Roger Hutchins is an Inclusion Manager at a junior school in Portsmouth.

Improving Pupil Motivation Together

Teachers and teaching assistants working collaboratively

Susan Bentham and
Roger Hutchins

 Routledge
Taylor & Francis Group

LONDON AND NEW YORK

First published 2012
by Routledge
2 Park Square, Milton Park, Abingdon, Oxon OX14 4RN

Simultaneously published in the USA and Canada
by Routledge
711 Third Avenue, New York, NY 10017

Routledge is an imprint of the Taylor & Francis Group, an informa business

British Library Cataloguing in Publication Data
A catalogue record for this book is available from the British Library

Library of Congress Cataloging in Publication Data
Bentham, Susan, 1958–
    Improving pupil motivation together : teachers and teaching assistants working
    collaboratively / Susan Bentham and Roger Hutchins.
        pages cm
    Includes bibliographical references and index.
    1. Motivation in education. 2. Teaching teams. 3. Teachers–In-service training.
    4. Teachers' assistants--In-service training. 5. Effective teaching. I. Hutchins, Roger,
    1953– II. Title.
    LB1065.B44 2012
    370.15'4–dc23   2011052006

ISBN: 978–0–415–58467–8 (hbk)
ISBN: 978–0–415–58469–2 (pbk)
ISBN: 978–0–203–11750–7 (ebk)

Typeset in Galliard
by Swales & Willis Ltd, Exeter, Devon

MIX
Paper from
responsible sources
FSC www.fsc.org   FSC® C004839

Printed and bound in Great Britain by
TJ International Ltd, Padstow, Cornwall

Contents

Illustrations

Tables

Case studies

Acknowledgements

Susan Bentham would like to thank the many students who have inspired this book and those teachers and teaching assistants who participated in her research.

Roger Hutchins gratefully acknowledges the continued support and encouragement of his wife, Anne, and the willing involvement of staff and pupils at his school, who have given their time and energy to provide him with invaluable insights into their experiences of education.

Introduction

This book is about many things. Primarily, it is about motivation: the motivation to engage, the motivation to learn and the motivation to behave in order to learn. The book assumes that a teacher and teaching assistant working together collaboratively can achieve more than either can achieve individually.

Theories of learning and motivation are complex and, as such, imaginary case studies are used throughout the book to illustrate points and to encourage thought and reflection. Theories regarding motivation and learning are interesting in their own right but, to make a difference in the classroom, the reader will need to actively think about how they can relate these theories to the pupils with whom they work.

This book is also informed by original research carried out by the authors for their respective doctoral studies. Sue Bentham carried out research to explore teachers' and teaching assistants' perceptions of collaborative relationships, while Roger Hutchins conducted research with junior school children about factors which influence pupil levels of motivation. In accordance with research protocols, names and details have been changed to ensure confidentiality.

Although there are now myriad support staff in schools (with numerous titles including teaching assistant, classroom assistant, special needs assistant, learning support assistant, HLTA and learning mentor, to mention just a few), the title that is used for consistency throughout this book is that of 'teaching assistant'.

Many adjectives have been used to describe pupils who seem to lack the motivation to engage, learn and behave. Newspaper headlines have referred to 'feral children' and to disengaged and disaffected youth. However, the challenge for those involved in education is how to inspire in pupils a real desire and passion for learning as well as an appreciation that learning can transform one's life – and that learning how to learn is a skill that is needed to function and thrive in society.

It is hoped that this book will be part of the debate on how to improve teaching and learning.

Chapter 1

What is education for?

An overview

This chapter begins with a story.

The way I see it

Rebekah is a junior school teacher of many years standing. As she looks back over the classes she has taught, she comments about how children learn differently:

> There are some children who learn in a straightforward way, children who understand that they can develop themselves and they want to learn. They can learn because they're interested in what they've done. They're interested in listening to our reason for doing it and they will attempt to do what we suggest. If you give them feedback, they are keen to learn and to respond to it. Other children still think they come to school and teachers do things to them, and then their teachers mark their work. They might have a look at it, but they hope that they can just forget about it and carry on with their lives.

> It's difficult to tell where their attitude to work comes from – how much is their personality? Does their approach to learning come from their home, or from the fact that they've just switched off from the way that we teach them?

What is Rebekah saying when she makes these comments?

For sure, the main focus seems to be on the different personal traits of children which cause them to respond in various ways to school. But reading 'underneath' her comments, as it were, are words and terms that she uses which need to be unpacked and looked at carefully. 'Feedback', for instance, is one of those words, and will be considered more fully in Chapter 2 (p. 39) of this book. 'Attitude' is another – and some consideration will be given to this later in this book. For this chapter, the key term to look at is 'learning'. Rebekah, along with every other school teacher, teaching assistant, parent and child in the country talks about 'learning' a lot – but what does she mean by 'learning'? What does *anyone* mean by 'learning'? If we are to investigate something about motivating pupils to *learn*, then we need to come to an understanding of what learning is, or could be. And, if we are talking about teachers and teaching assistants collaborating together in that learning process, then it is especially important that teachers and assistants mean the same thing when they use that term.

One of the defining characteristics of what it is to be human is that humans have to *learn* to survive and develop – and a major way we learn is by being taught. Learning does not happen merely by imitation or through personal experience, and much of human learning takes place in schools. School is the place in which young humans experience 'education'. In this chapter we consider some of the purposes of such an education.

What is education for?

Children, by and large, are genetically hard-wired to learn. Young children are motivated to play, to learn to walk and run, to investigate their environment. They do not need to be told to look around them, to crawl, to make choices, to explore their immediate world. It takes an awful lot to entirely crush that instinctive and natural desire for knowledge and fresh experience. One of the tragedies of famine, serious illness or trauma can be seen in news pictures of children's faces totally devoid of interest or desire.

Motivation in relation to schooling, however, is something different. In school we want children to be motivated to learn something imposed on them from outside – something they have not directly or consciously chosen to do. This process began, for them, a long time before they started school. They have, for instance, been taught how to use the toilet, how to eat with implements rather than fingers, how to get dressed and washed and how to say 'please' and 'thank you'. These are not things the young infants choose for themselves and, as any parent knows, these are by no means easy or straightforward skills to learn. The motivation to respond positively to training and requests can be decidedly lacking in toddlers. However, by and large, pre-school children spend their days in activities which, hopefully, are generally pleasurable and most, but by no means all, are ready for school by the time that they are old enough to attend.

And here is the rub. It is an all-too-truism to state that by the age of five children can't wait to start school but by the age of fifteen they can't wait to leave. Of course, this is a gross generalisation and over-simplification of a complex process, but there is enough truth in it to warrant attention.

As one primary school teacher put it:

> *I feel like children intrinsically want to learn and that during the course of their twelve years at school we batter that desire out of a lot of them.*

What has happened?

A key factor is the *purpose* of education and, in particular, the views held by classroom or subject teachers and teaching assistants themselves. Why does a teacher teach? Why does a teaching assistant assist? What do they think they are doing when they engage in these activities? On a day-to-day basis, most time is taken up with the business of schooling – the curriculum, the timetable, planning, marking, responding to challenging behaviours and the like. Thinking about *why* to educate children in the first place can easily be seen as an irrelevant luxury: 'We've *got* to do it and we've only enough time and energy to get on with the job at hand – never mind all this educational theory nonsense.'

Various views on the purpose of education

But, whether we think about it or not, everyone has some kind of view about why children go to school. Here might be some of them:

- Children need to learn in order to prepare them for adult life.
- Children go to school to learn to get on with others.
- Children are in school to expand their horizons.
- Children attend class to grow in wisdom and understanding.
- I send my children to school to get them out of my hair!

Much of the time we do not think about the *why* of school because there is no choice – school is a fact of life and has been for many generations. But it has not always been like this and it is not like this in many parts of the world.

What does motivation have to do with education?

This chapter attempts to 'lift the lid' on teachers' and teaching assistants' views and understandings of the purpose of education. It tries to get underneath the taken-for-granted aspects of school life and to question and examine underlying principles and perspectives. The reason for this is straightforward: when teachers and teaching assistants talk about how motivated or not pupils are – for instance, saying things like 'Jimmy is just not interested in school work'– they have in mind something called 'learning', but they may not have thought through just what they mean by 'learning'. This chapter attempts to help teachers and teaching assistants think through various aspects of what is, or could be, meant by learning.

Thinking about the reasons for, and the purposes of, education is important and needs to be considered before we enter into a discussion of motivation itself – because motivation is always related to a purpose. Motivation is towards a goal. When we say we are motivated, we are motivated to do or achieve *something*. We cannot be motivated simply to be motivated. So, if we are considering motivation for education, we need to be clear about what we mean by words like 'education', 'schooling' and 'learning'. If the goal of motivation is learning, both teachers and teaching assistants need to be clear about what learning 'looks like'. This is part of our thinking when we ask such questions as 'What do we want children to learn in this lesson?', 'How will we know when children have learned what we want them to learn?' and 'How is learning measured?' All of these questions have to do with motivation, for how we answer them will determine both how we teach and what expectations we will have of our pupils. Motivation is always towards a goal – and we now consider some different 'goals' or purposes of education.

Differing purposes of education

Schools fail our pupils yet again
Exclusion rates up for the second year in a row
One third of children leave junior school not being able to read or write
Grammar is not taught any more
Exam levels are going up – but are the exams getting easier?
Parents up in arms at school closure
Pupils' delight at GCSE results
More 'A stars' than ever before
Standards across the country have improved

These are some imaginary news headlines – but they reflect the tone of much media reporting in the papers, television and radio. A quick read should leave you confused – are schools 'failing' or are they 'succeeding'?

The answer to the question is not clear-cut, but must have something to do with why schools are there. What do people, including the media, think schools are for? It is very easy to take the answer for granted, as though it were obvious and 'natural'. Yet there is nothing 'natural' about it – different cultures and different times have expressed different reasons for the purpose of schools, and schools are judged as being 'successful' or 'failing' according to why people think they exist.

In this section, we outline some of the reasons that people have used, in different places and in different times, to justify the existence of schools.

An idealistic vision

Education is there to make children fully 'human'. Morality, character, lifestyle (the virtues) are placed on equal par with knowledge, insight and information. Education is for everyone because everyone is an individual with the potential for personal and academic development. Diversity and equality are regarded as essential rights. The aim of education is to instil the young of a society with the values of virtue and justice. In this way, the good of society and the good of the individual will be mutually established.

Teaching the faith

Schooling is a means of educating all children 'in the ways of God'. Parents and teachers together teach children the religious traditions of their society in such a way that their view of history and of current earthly affairs is shaped by their understanding of the divine purpose of the world.

Religious elitism

Formal education is reserved for an elite group of pupils to be taught rigid dogma in order that they might grow up to become the scribes of the state religion. Schooling is not for the benefit of the pupils, but for the preservation of society.

Political indoctrination

Schools are there to train children according to strict political and social ideologies. Children are given a narrow view of history and of the world, usually from an extreme nationalistic perspective. No deviation is permitted from the official view either in the school or in the home. Such schooling may well be given exclusively in the dominant language of the state.

Humanistic enlightenment

Education is seen as a human right. Schooling is to promote knowledge and discovery. Education is a 'natural', inalienable right for all children. Ignorance is not bliss – those without knowledge are disadvantaged in a 'knowledge society'. Education is not to equip children to perform a specific role within adult society, neither is it to force a particular religious or moral ideology on them. Rather it is to educate for freedom; the idea being to provide children with an understanding of a wide range of perspectives and values so they can choose for themselves the 'right' way to live. Children are encouraged to be open-minded, tolerant and inclusive.

Democratic education

Educating children is a human right, but it comes with responsibilities. Education is not merely for the benefit and development of the individual child, but also for the development and betterment of a free and fair society. Children are to be educated to prepare them to live in freedom in a free society. Virtues such as tolerance, respect and understanding are to be consciously taught to pupils alongside a formal academic curriculum.

Utilitarian/functional education

Formal education costs a great deal, and whoever pays for it should get something in return: 'value for money' is essential. Governments pay for education through taxation and, therefore, governments say what education is for. Formal schooling is provided in order to render children fit for 'society' and 'work', and thus to produce people who can contribute to, perpetuate and help secure the future of the state. Education must be 'fit for purpose'. A curriculum is to be followed, rather than knowledge to be explored. Teachers are to be held to account for what they teach. Children are to be examined to ensure they are learning what is deemed to be essential for their future employment and to show that the investment in their education in terms of time and money has not been wasted. Gaining recognised and certificated qualifications, normally through sitting formal examinations, is seen as the end product of education.

Discussion points

a.   Which approach do you think the education system in England today most reflects?
b.   What do you think are likely implications of these varying views on educational practices?
c.   What do *you* think should be the purpose of education?

What does it mean to learn?

Whatever the purpose of education, education has to do with 'learning', and this book is about motivation for *learning*. However, 'learning', like 'education', is a taken-for-granted phrase. Along with much else in education, it is assumed that everyone understands what learning is and that all are in agreement about it. The term 'learning' is used all the time in school and is such a familiar aspect of the fabric of educational life that it is probably very rarely thought about in schools and classes. But there are many different theories of learning, and each theory impacts on the teaching style, teaching methods and expectations of pupils held by teachers and teaching assistants – and all of this has an enormous impact and influence on pupil motivation.

Case study 1.1: 'What's the point of this?'

In a year 10 history class, the keen young teacher (Mr Johnson) is trying to get his class to look at the origins of the First World War from a number of different angles.

Mr Johnson: I am going to split the class into four groups. I want you all to look at the books and websites I've set you and I want you to think about why the First World War happened. But I want each group to do it in a slightly different way. I would like Group 1 to think about how Britain viewed the events leading up to the outbreak of war. Group 2, look at it from Germany's point of view; Group 3 from how Russia saw it, and Group 4 to find out how these events were seen in America. Is that clear?

At the back of the class sits Robert. Robert is not too impressed.

Robert: Sir. What's the point of all this? I just want to know the answer.

Sitting near Robert is Miss Trumpington. She is a teaching assistant who helps Robert with his school work. She does not say anything out loud, but is thinking 'All Robert needs to know is how to read and write; and he'll need a whole lot of support just to do that. Why should he be bothered about all this history stuff anyway? He's not going to need it when he leaves school in a year's time.'

What is happening? Before reading on, it might be worth you thinking about this for yourself. How would you describe the dynamics in this classroom?

In this imaginary case study, the teacher holds a view about what learning is that is considerably at odds with how the pupil understands learning. Mr Johnson wants to expand his students' minds and get them to see that historical events can be viewed in different ways. Robert simply wants to get the class over and done with, and Miss Trumpington has her eye on Robert's future prospects. In this classroom, then, there are at least three different views of the purpose of education:

- Opening pupils' minds and expanding their horizons.
- A task to complete, or at least, to get through.
- A place to be equipped for life outside of school.

These differing views could potentially lead to tension and possible conflict within the classroom between these three people. They will each be motivated to do different things and be tempted to think that what the others are motivated to do is of less importance than their considerations and, indeed, may not be worthwhile at all.

The following sections of this chapter are given so that teachers and teaching assistants can reflect on and discuss together their own views and assumptions regarding learning.

Learning equates with thinking

It could be argued that, if learning is about anything, it is about developing thinking. Yet this is not necessarily a straightforward concept. The Mission Statement of one school is 'learn to think – think to learn', seemingly equating learning with thinking. But this statement begs the question: What does it mean to think?

Consider the following scenarios:

Are the class thinking?
In a classroom, the teacher stands at the front and asks the class: 'What is 3 multiplied by 7?'

The children respond: '21.'

Are the class thinking? It depends both on the age of the children and their prior knowledge. If this question was being asked of a top maths set in year 6 or students preparing for GCSE maths, the class are not going to be thinking – their response is automatic. They *know* it – or at least, they should! Asking the same questions of a year 1 class might be very different. Some of the children may know the answer by rote, but most may well have to work it out – they would have to engage in *thinking*.

Again, a teacher might put this instruction on a board for the class to complete:

Fill in the missing letters: a, b, c, _, _, f. . .

Whether the children are thinking or not, as they respond to this, depends on their level of knowledge and understanding. If fourteen-year-old students were to be given this instruction they almost certainly will not need to think about the answer – they *know* it – but for a child in a nursery or reception class, learning their alphabet for the first time, the situation is entirely different. In order to answer the question, the child has to engage in thinking. And, as thinking takes place so learning occurs. New facts are learned and remembered. New ways of looking at the world are encountered. Changes occur to the child's brain and to the child's understanding of, and outlook on, the world.

In this context, motivating pupils to learn therefore has to do with motivating them to *think* – to work with their brain, their experience and their existing knowledge all whilst interacting with the physical environment of the class, with other children in their class and with the adults in the class – the teacher and the teaching assistants. Motivating pupils to *think* is a key part of learning – but herein lies a difficulty. How do you know what a child is thinking? Consider the following scenarios.

What were you thinking about?

Teacher: 'What were you thinking of?' (to a pupil who has climbed on the shed roof in the playground to collect his football or to a pupil who has punched another pupil in the face).

Mother: 'What were you thinking about?' (to a child who has run into the road and nearly been knocked over by a car).

A possible answer from them is that they were not consciously thinking about anything, so a response of shrugging shoulders, anger or crying is likely. Thinking can be unconscious as well as conscious.

Alternatively, they could each have been thinking very specifically, in a focused way with a tunnel-vision which excluded all other considerations: to get my ball back; to get the pupil back; to get to the other side of the road.

Children can rarely give a logical, well thought-out answer when asked why they lashed out, threw chairs, hit others, or refused to do their work. Normally, they cannot give a reason: 'I dunno' is a response guaranteed to wind up both a teacher and a mother.

Sometimes, however, children who do things like this *do* have a clear reason for doing it – and it is to do with motivation.

The boy climbing the shed roof may have carefully thought about it and weighed up the risks, taking account of his ability to scale drainpipes, his experience with roof climbing and the likelihood of getting caught. He was motivated to get his ball back, and he knew he could do it.

The pupil's act of landing a punch on the other's nose may have been premeditated and deliberate – getting his own back for being picked on. He was motivated by revenge or justice (depending on your point of view) and he planned for it.

The child crossing the road may have looked both ways and seen the car, but thought it was going more slowly than it was, misjudging the danger. She was motivated by her desire to get across the road to what was on the other side and had, in her thinking, taken all necessary precautions.

It is not always possible to tell what children are thinking, and what their motivation might be, by looking solely at their actions.

When considering motivation, it is not enough to simply look at what a pupil is doing – you need to talk with them to find out what is making them tick. Remember – motivation is always towards a goal. The pupils may not be able to articulate exactly what their motivation was, but talking with them should give some kind of clue about their thought processes.

However, 'learning' involves more than 'thinking', as we will now discuss.

Theories of learning as happening within a social context

A theory is a way of looking at the world: it helps us to understand, interpret and make sense of it. Below, we consider three theories which view learning as being more than merely 'thinking'. The purpose is not to say 'this is what learning is', but to provide food for thought to teachers and teaching assistants, for it is only as we reflect on our views and practices that our teaching and our engagement with pupils (and therefore with their motivation) will develop.

Teachers and teaching assistants who hold any one of these views of learning will go about their job differently from those who hold a different view. They will see their pupils, their role, and even see themselves in different lights. They may not have a choice over *what* is taught, as this is laid down in a set curriculum, but they certainly do have a choice over *how* it is taught and how they organise the classroom and talk with the pupils. And how they go about this will, in large measure, be determined by what view they hold about what learning actually is.

Learning as thinking is based on a view that children primarily learn in isolation from each other and from the world around them. Here, learning is conceived, taught, assessed and judged in purely individual terms. The theories considered below challenge this view of learning. All three theories, although distinctive, hold one theme in common – children learn, not in isolation from the world, adults or each other, but rather learning takes place socially, in some kind of community.

The theories of learning we will consider are those of:

- Jerome Bruner – learning and culture (*The Culture of Education,* 1996).
- Ference Marton and Shirley Booth – learning as experience (*Learning and Awareness,* 1997).
- Etienne Wenger – learning as social participation (*Communities of Practice,* 1998).

Jerome Bruner (1996)

Scaffolding learning and the spiral curriculum

Bruner is probably best known for his concepts of the 'spiral curriculum' and 'scaffolding' learning. These ideas have been around in schools for many years. Essentially the 'spiral curriculum' means that children can be taught at many levels. In the beginning it is simply for them to grasp initial concepts, and then, through the years, they revisit that same subject area several times, each time learning more complex things. 'Scaffolding' learning means providing supports to aid learning which are later removed when that particular aspect has been learnt. This can be as simple as providing line guides when children are learning to write.

In his later writing, Bruner says that in his original theories of learning he focused purely on individual learning processes and did not pay enough attention to the social context in which children's learning takes place. He now argues that education cannot be considered in isolation from the wider culture in which the schools exist. Indeed, education is an integral part of culture; culture both shapes, and is itself shaped by, education. From this perspective, children learn within the context of culture – the immediate culture of their family, their locality, their school, and the wider culture of society at large. As Bruner comments, 'Mental life is lived with others' (p. xi).

Meaning making

For Bruner, learning is not about a child individually learning facts and increasing in knowledge; it is about children as groups, along with their teachers, engaging in what he terms 'meaning making'. By this he means developing an interpretation, an understanding of, and a connection with, the wider culture. Such a development may not be conscious or deliberate – but nevertheless this is something that takes place.

An illustration of this may be helpful. Let us go back to the case study of the history lesson on the origins of the First World War. As the lesson progresses, the students settle to their tasks and then report back their findings. They come to see that there is no straightforward answer to the question, 'Why did the First World War happen?' They begin to realise that different nations held differing views and that even within those nations lots of people held very differing views. So far, so good. They have learnt something about history. But is this *all* they have learned? In Bruner's terms, some of them may also have taken on board a view that, if this was the case with the First World War, it may also apply today to similar situations. There is no right or wrong way of looking at conflict in the world today – it all depends on your perspective. In this instance, these students have 'made meaning' about the world in which they live. And that 'meaning' has occurred as a result of the education they have experienced in that lesson.

To recap: in this lesson, pupils may have learnt something at a number of different 'levels' (if you will). At the most basic level, students will have learnt some facts. Pupils at this level may simply want someone to 'tell them the answer'. At the next level, other students will have begun to learn that different people viewed the same events from very different points of view – for example, Britain saw the war as being caused by German aggression, but Germans saw it as defending their homeland. Students at this level of learning have begun to learn that there *is* no right answer, so no one can tell it to them. But other students may have attained a further level of learning which could relate to what Bruner terms 'meaning making'. Here, students have learnt 'facts' and 'perspectives' that they now begin to apply (consciously or unconsciously) to what they have learnt in their own lives and contexts. They begin to see that there are different perspectives to conflicts which occur today. They begin to see that there is rarely a right or wrong answer to questions facing politicians and governments in the world today. Through their education they have begun to 'make meaning' of the culture around them. As their realisation and understanding of past events deepens, they create their own understandings of the world in which they themselves live; it begins to make sense to them in a new way. They are able to generalise what they have learnt in the classroom to other situations – in other words, they have begun to 'make meaning' of the culture in which they live.

Self-identity

As well as 'meaning making', a key factor in Bruner's argument is that schools are hugely significant in the development of the concept of 'Self' (the way pupils view themselves as learners in school – 'learner identity').

At this point, it might be worth you jotting down a few notes or words about your own school days. What immediately comes to mind when you think about yourself in class? Some may write 'swot', others 'struggler'. Alternatives might be 'enjoyment', 'failure', 'belonging' or 'alienation'. All of these are words to do with identity – how we think and feel about ourselves when we are in the context of learning. This can, of course, be different for different subjects and different in the presence of different teachers or classmates. Many motivational theorists focus on this sense of 'self' and 'identity' – Bruner's thinking has clear links with attribution theory (pp. 34–36).

Bruner asks where that sense of 'self' comes from in school. For some pupils, it may come from the subject being taught: 'I am successful because I am good at maths' or 'I am a failure because I can't get the hang of chemistry.' But, for most, it comes through how teachers and teaching assistants act towards them. In the development of his theory of learning, Bruner talks of the 'underground curriculum'. This is what is happening beneath the surface of the classroom and it influences pupils and their motivation possibly more than the obvious curriculum which is being taught. One way in which this 'underground curriculum' is shown, Bruner says, is in teachers' attitudes towards pupils.

Going back to the case study of the history lesson, Mr Johnson views his pupils as being capable of finding out for themselves; as being able to work together to explain their ideas and to learn from each other. Another teacher with another attitude might have stood in front of the class and lectured them about the First World War, expecting them to take notes and to sit quietly and take in the wisdom and knowledge he was giving them.

How would you describe this last teacher's attitude towards his pupils?

Bruner argues that the 'underground curriculum' can, perhaps, most obviously be seen in a school's approach to assessment, which in itself is one of the key ways learner identity is shaped:

- 'Success and failure are principal nutrients of the development of selfhood' (Bruner 1996, p. 36).
- 'School judges the child's performance and the child responds by evaluating himself or herself in turn.'
- The self 'increasingly takes on the flavour of these evaluations' (p. 37).

Tests and exams hold dread or expectation (or perhaps a mixture of both) for many students, and they view themselves as learners in the light of the results of these tests.

- One pupil could view herself as a 'successful' learner.
- Another could see herself as essentially a 'failure'.

Both pupils have been taught the same way by the same teachers, but they got very different results in their exams. Bruner argues that how a school or how teachers handle those sorts of pressures goes a long way towards helping shape pupil identity.

Case study 1.2: A class charter

Diane Avon is a year 5 teacher. It is the first week of the new academic year and she wants to establish the 'feel' of the classroom as a positive learning environment which will promote the learning of each pupil in her class. In this particular session she is talking with the class about a 'class charter'.

She asks the pupils to sit in a circle on the carpet at the front of the room and puts up a slide on the interactive white board (IWB). At the top is the title: 'A class charter'. She asks the class what they think a 'charter' is. Several pupils make their suggestions. Diane puts the next slide up: 'A charter is an agreement of rights and responsibilities.'

She now shows the slide which reads:

What rights do we feel we need in 5A?

What responsibilities do we feel we have in 5A?

She gives a few ideas to the class, saying things like 'I will always respect you' and 'In 5A we are all equal and we have the right to be equal. A lot of rights and responsibilities are to do with fairness.' She then asks the class to talk about this amongst themselves, saying to them 'I'm asking you to do something now that is very, very hard. What do you think you should have a right to in 5A? It's going to take some real taxing of our brains.'

She sends the class back to their tables to talk and to see if they can write their ideas down. After ten minutes or so, she calls the class back to the carpet and puts another slide up on the IWB showing them what she herself has thought of:

You have the right to be yourself
To speak and be heard without interruption
To work without interference
Respect
A healthy and safe learning environment
Equal opportunities
To ask questions
To receive stimulating answers
To make mistakes without being ridiculed
To be supported so that you can learn to the best of your ability

Diane elaborates on the last points:

'I want you to ask questions in year 5. I will answer you if I can. I want to give answers that make you think. If I don't know the answer (and I don't know everything) I'll find out for you.

'Being ridiculed means being made fun of. We are all human, we all make mistakes. Making mistakes is an important part of learning. Actually, making mistakes is good for learning.

'You have the right to come and say to me "I think I need this".'

She goes on to say that with rights come responsibilities: 'We are all responsible to ensure we can all receive these rights.'

She says to the class that she will collect the ideas they have written down and go through them with them at the next PSHE lesson, so that they draw up a charter between them with which everyone is happy.

In this lesson, we see an example of Bruner's 'underground curriculum' in action. The teacher shows a very positive attitude towards the pupils – they are important to her and they are important to each other. She places herself within, rather than on top of or somehow outside, their learning community. Whether they are conscious of it or not, in this environment the pupils are learning what it means to live and learn within a democratic culture.

Motivation to learn within this classroom is likely to be high!

Ference Marton and Shirley Booth (1997)

Learning as experience

Marton and Booth developed their theories of learning from work undertaken over many years in Sweden and Hong Kong. For them, the key issue is one of *experience*: 'We . . . describe learning in terms of the experience of learning, or learning as coming to experience the world in one way or another' (p. 33). Such experience changes the person; thus learning equals change. If some change in the person does not take place, then genuine learning has not taken place.

They distinguish between two types of learning – *surface learning* and *deep learning*.

Surface learning

Surface learning treats learning as something external to the learner; a task to perform, such as gathering facts and information, which is taken in from the outside. Learning here is equated with increasing in knowledge, but such knowledge is really mere information – nothing happens as a result of it to the person. When faced with 'getting through' exams, pupils will often engage only in surface learning – getting a grip on 'facts' which enables them to pass the test but which are forgotten soon afterwards. Just like water running off a duck's back, such learning really is only 'surface' deep – it doesn't get underneath the skin, as it were.

Case study 1.3: 'Hutchins, I despair of you!'

'Hutchins, I despair of you!'

The frustrated cry of my year 10 French teacher still lingers in my memory, even though it was many, many years ago. I was not unintelligent. I was doing alright in most subjects and very well in a few. Languages, however, eluded me and I struggled. Indeed, I really gave up trying. No wonder that Miss got frustrated. But why did I give up? One reason relates, I believe, to Marton and Booth's arguments – French had no meaning in my world; it was outside my experience. The only contact I had with it was a couple of lessons a week – it was truly surface learning. In the event, I did what was necessary and scraped a pass at 'O' level – but I am still unable to converse with a French speaker.

Deep learning

Deep learning, however, is a means of finding out and connecting with the reality of the world around us. Such learners 'see learning as changing ourself in some way' (p. 35). The main idea here is 'enlightenment, seeing things in a new light' (p. 37). We might say that 'the penny has dropped'. Deep learning can only take place when learners are able to place what they are being taught in the context of their experience of the world. 'Genuine learning always relates to the learner's reality, the world as already experienced' (p. 140). If what is being taught is somehow isolated or divorced from the learner's experience of the world, that learning is likely to fail. An example of deep learning could be as obvious as learning to ride a bicycle or learning to swim – 'once learnt, never forgotten' as the saying goes. The person who has learnt to ride a bike or learnt to swim has his or her life changed – they now ride bicycles or go for a swim. The person who has only learnt *about* riding or swimming has not had their life changed at all.

An individual pupil can hold one or other of these approaches when it comes to learning but, perhaps more significantly, a teacher can also hold either one of these approaches. A teacher who is satisfied with merely 'surface' learning will teach very differently to one who is concerned that her pupils experience 'deep' learning.

But is 'surface learning' always less appropriate than 'deep learning'? Does deep learning always trump surface learning? The answer is not straightforward. As one adult remembers:

Looking back on my early school days I vividly remember learning my times tables. As a class we would stand and chant for hours 'seven times seven equals forty-nine' and the

Case study 1.4: Deep learning

A teacher looks back on his own education. He recalls how 'deep learning' occurred for him in mathematics:

> I remember it vividly. It was in my third year of secondary school. Maths had never been my strong point. I had always just 'got by', learning things parrot-fashion but not really understanding it. Then we did 'relative velocity'. The teacher told us to imagine two trains, each going at 70 miles per hour. One train was travelling northwards and the other southwards. As they passed each other, the relative velocity would be 140 miles per hour (two lots of 70 miles per hour added together) – in practical terms this meant that a person sitting in one of the carriages would pass a second person sitting in a carriage on the other train at 140 miles per hour. Suddenly it all made sense. If you like, it was a 'Eureka' moment. I could understand this, and from then on, for some reason, every other aspect of maths slotted into place.

For this teacher, 'deep learning' was taking place. And this type of learning changed not only his thinking, but the way he looked at the world and the way he looked at himself. For him, learning really did equal experience.

---

rest of the seven times table, or whichever one it happened to be. Every now and then the teacher would stop us and demand that 'so and so' answer what was six times seven or whatever. It was a drill. It was rote learning. But it kept us on our toes and to this day, some fifty years on, I still know my times tables!

This seems like surface learning – but it enabled that person to get to grips with other 'deeper' learning later on in life. It would seem, therefore, that there may be a place, after all, for surface learning!

Etienne Wenger (1998)

Wenger focuses on two major aspects of learning – learning 'together' and learner 'identity'.

Communities of practice

For Wenger, learning takes place within what he calls a 'community of practice'. He questions the view that 'learning is an individual process, that it has a beginning and an end, that it is best separated from the rest of our activities and that it is the result of teaching' (p. 3). He argues that this view of education is misdirected and results in much of the teaching in schools being perceived and experienced as being irrelevant: 'Most of us come out of this treatment feeling that learning is boring and arduous, and that we are not really cut out for it' (p. 3).

He poses an alternative view of what learning actually is: 'Learning is essentially a social phenomenon, reflecting our deeply social nature as human beings capable of knowing'

(p. 3). In his thinking, communities of practice can occur in many situations – families, work places, school classrooms, school playgrounds – but they do not inevitably occur in any of those places. A community of practice has to have certain specific aspects if it is to be a place of genuine learning:

- It is made up of *participants* who *belong* and *identify* with other members of that community of practice.
- A community of practice arises when the members of the community actively and consciously work with each other – what Wenger calls *mutual engagement*, i.e. there is a process of 'give and take'.
- It is a *joint enterprise* – no one person is responsible for what happens with the rest passively following on. Each member shares responsibility for the whole thing.
- Members of it experience a *shared repertoire* (by which is meant, shared routines, vocabulary, ways of doing things).

Participation

For Wenger, 'participation' is a really important word and involves considerably more than what is commonly understood by the term. 'Participation', in Wenger's thinking, requires the engagement of the whole person (feelings, will and mind), his or her imagination (a sense of what participants might become) and alignment of that person's values with the values of the community (the values of the community of practice become *my* values).

Learner identity

Out of this participation comes 'identity' – which is another crucial aspect of Wenger's theory: 'Because learning transforms who we are and what we can do, it is an experience of identity. It is not just an accumulation of skills and information, but a process of becoming' (p. 215). A participant must *identify* with the community of practice and he or she must see themselves as *members* of that community. Identity is shaped both by participation and non-participation – what we do *not* join as much shapes our identity as what we *do* join.

Case study 1.5: Community of practice? Version 1

In a year 6 class, the teacher (Miss Pitcher) is organising the class so that students may continue their history topic on the Tudors. She asks the class to clear away what they have previously been doing and come and sit in front of her on the carpet. While the class does this, John sulkily looks at one of the class displays with his back to the rest of the children. After a minute or so the class are now sat on the carpet in front of Miss Pitcher – all but John. John is sitting on the floor by himself at the back of the class, leaning against a cupboard and looking very miserable. He has had an altercation of some sort with a supply teacher during the morning and has chosen to sit away from the rest of the class.

Miss Pitcher tells the class they are to write notes about yesterday's class visit to local spots of Tudor interest. As a stimulus to this activity, she shows photographs she took of her group on yesterday's visit. She asks the class to watch quietly the first time through, just to refresh their own memories and gather their thoughts about the visit. They are then to talk in pairs about their own memories and thoughts about the trip before they make their notes. All of those sitting on the carpet respond to this and all are animated in their discussions. There is a general hum of conversation within the room.

However, John is still sitting at the back of the class by himself. He stares down at his feet and mutters, 'I'll just talk to the floor, then'. He then immediately repeats this out loud. Miss Pitcher beckons him forward and they talk one-to-one for a bit about his memories of the trip.

While this is happening, three girls (Ruth, Esther and Angela) have moved to sit next to each other and are now comparing jewellery – they are each wearing lockets around their necks. During the teacher's instruction, Ruth spent at least half of the time not looking at the board; instead she was looking at her two friends, who are not supposed to sit next to each other. Now they are sitting a little away from the main body of the pupils, and they are not focused on the task at all.

What is happening in this classroom? Using Wenger's term – is this class a community of practice or is it something different? What do you think?

In the case of Miss Pitcher's class, the answer to the question 'Is the class a community of practice?' is that it depends on who we are talking about. There seems to be a community of practice for the majority of the pupils – those who actively participate in the activity – and, for some of the time, it seems to exist for three of the pupils – Ruth, Esther and Angela – who were possibly participating at the beginning, but certainly were not by the end. For John, the class was never a community of practice. However, the teacher, by initiating an individual conversation with John, was seeking to draw him into that community and help him find a sense of belonging.

Constellations of communities of practice

According to Wenger, a school cannot in itself be a community of practice because it is too big and diverse; it can, however, constitute a 'constellation' of a number of communities of practice. A class *can* be a community of practice, though sometimes it is not necessarily a successful community. For a whole class to be a community of practice, all of the pupils must view themselves as participants. They must see themselves as learners, but learners *within that community*. They are actively *involved* in the class, which is more than simply turning up and sitting at their places for the required amount of hours.

Opportunity rather than compulsion

Teachers cannot force pupils to become participants in a community of practice, but they can create the conditions which allow for and promote such participation. If we go back to the case study of Diane Avon and her 'class charter', we can see that she is beginning to create the conditions for a community of practice to be established in her class. In Wenger's terminology, she is actively encouraging each pupil to 'participate' in class; to take on an identity of a 'learner within the community of learners' that is class 5A. In another part of the lesson, she encourages the pupils to see themselves as being 'a bridge to one another's learning'. This is an example of seeking to establish learning as a social rather than as an isolated experience.

But what if a teacher went about this a different way?

Case study 1.6: Community of practice? Version 2

Mildred Downcast is a year 5 teacher. It is the first week of the new academic year and she wants to establish the feel of the classroom – a learning environment which will promote the good behaviour and well-ordered learning of her class. She is talking with the class about a 'class charter'. The pupils are sitting in rows in front of her while she paces up and down lecturing them. The interactive whiteboard is not in use; instead she speaks to them about her expectations for the coming year:

> This is a new year. It is a time for a fresh start. I know some of you had a difficult time last year. This year will be different. I expect instant obedience. I expect you to listen to me and to pay attention. I do *not* want to see fidgeting. I do *not* expect to hear whispering. When I am speaking, you will listen and you will learn.
>
> We have been told that we have to have a class charter – whatever that means. Here are the responsibilities I expect you to have.
>
> You are each responsible for your own learning; you cannot rely on anyone else.
>
> You will each do your homework and bring it in on time.
>
> You will do the work I set you; otherwise you will stay in and miss your breaks until it is finished.
>
> I will help you with your work, but I will only help you when I have seen that you have worked at it first and tried your best.

She carries on in this vein for ten minutes and then goes on to give the class a spelling test and a maths test.

One suspects that Miss Downcast's class is unlikely to develop into one of Wenger's communities of practice! Her teaching style and her attitudes towards the pupils (again linked to Bruner's 'underground curriculum') would seem likely to prevent her class becoming a community of practice.

Case study 1.7: What is this community of practice?

Two teachers, Carol and Gerald, are reading Wenger's book. They are discussing his arguments that, based on his theory of learning, there are a number of problems with 'traditional' educational practices:

Carol: Listen to this quote: 'Competence . . . means pleasing the teacher, raising your hand first, getting good grades. It is no surprise then . . . that some students either seek their identity in subversive behaviour or simply refuse to participate' (p. 269). Does he really mean it's wrong to get good grades or to show you know something by putting your hand up? To say these things are not important is ridiculous.

Gerald: I don't think Wenger means to say they are wrong in themselves. What I think he is trying to get at is that if that is *all* learning is about, pupils will not see it as being relevant to their lives outside of school. Some of them will feel OK about it, but many will not. And you've only got to look at how many kids get turned off school to see that he might have a point.

Carol: But what about this? He says that only a few pupils benefit from there being a fixed curriculum to follow. Schools have *always* had a curriculum to follow. There's got to be some agreement about what is to be taught in schools. I remember when I was in junior school – the teachers taught us what they wanted, which usually was what they themselves enjoyed and were good at. So one year I got loads of music and no science at all. No – there's got to be a curriculum that all schools keep to.

Gerald: Well, I agree, and I don't think Wenger disagrees. What I think he means is that when a school or a teacher follows a set curriculum rigidly without any deviation or taking the interests of the pupils into account then only a very few pupils will be interested enough to learn. These few pupils are likely to already value what is being taught and see it as being relevant to them – the majority of the pupils will simply see it as something imposed on them over which they have no say.

Carol: I also read that Wenger says that in a classroom where everybody is being expected to learn the same thing at the same time, there is no room for negotiation, no room for different learner identities to develop, no room for interdependent learning. Well, that's not like any classroom *I* know. Lessons *I've* seen have been differentiated with different levels of work being given to different groups of pupils. In many of the lessons pupils are given a *lot* of choice about what they do.

Gerald: In my reading of Wenger, he isn't saying that this is *necessarily* what happens in class. He is saying that *if* this is what happens – and all pupils are expected to work at the same thing in the same way and over the same time period – then many pupils will suffer and not be motivated to learn at all.

Carol: But he also writes that social relationships are mistrusted rather than being viewed as 'essential ingredients of learning in order to maximise the engagement of its members' (pp. 271–272). I take it that means he thinks friendships between pupils should be allowed; but I think they often get in the way of learning rather than helping it. I've had loads of pupils over the years who would spend all their time chatting if they could and would learn absolutely nothing. In my opinion social relationships *should* be mistrusted.

Gerald: I think Wenger is thinking about something more than simple friendship. I think he is talking about pupils learning together, helping each other learn rather than learning in isolation from each other. This is something the teacher can and should encourage. But it's always necessary to make sure the pupils really are learning rather than just chatting – as you say!

Carol: Well, maybe. But this last point Wenger makes is surely totally impractical in a classroom. He says that in traditional education students are not allowed to take charge or have any control over their own learning. So what? How can he think it could be otherwise? If he thinks we should let them take control, he's got another think coming.

Gerald: I agree that pupils cannot be in total control over what happens in class. It is the teacher's responsibility to teach and to teach what the pupils need to know. But I think Wenger is saying that pupils who have absolutely *no* say in what is being taught or how it is being taught are likely to be too demotivated to learn. They are more likely to see it as something imposed on them from the outside. Of course, there will always be the passive few who still think that learning is something that is 'done to them' who might like this form of teaching, but the majority will not. Whatever we think about Wenger's arguments, there is a lot of stuff to think about.

Carol: That's true. One thing I really do like about Wenger is when he says that a key element in encouraging a community of practice to emerge within a classroom is the teacher viewing themselves as being participating members of that community alongside their pupils. He writes this: 'It is not so much by the specific content of their pedagogy as by their status as members that they take part in generational encounter . . . Being an active practitioner with an authentic form of participation might be one of the most deeply essential requirements for teaching' (pp. 276–277). I agree with that and really try to see myself as being a part of the class alongside the pupils.

Gerald: So do I – so maybe we are not so different in our views after all!

Discussion points

a.   To what 'communities of practice' might pupils in a class belong?

b.   How would you be able to tell if a class was a 'community of practice' or not?

c.   How might a teacher and teaching assistant encourage a class to become a 'community of practice'?

Teachers' perceptions of their roles

As we shall discuss in Chapter 4, for pupils a key influence on their motivation (certainly in the primary phase of schooling) is the teacher. How teachers view themselves and their roles is therefore crucial in pupil motivation. We now turn to a consideration of how two junior school teachers perceive their role in the classroom.

My role as a teacher

Julia: To facilitate children's learning. To help them learn how to learn stuff. To teach them certain facts and then to enable them to learn things for themselves. I don't necessarily subscribe to the teacher at the front, just giving information old-style; but equally I don't necessarily subscribe to completely child-led exploratory learning. I think a bit of a mixture is the way forward. I like a class full of people who can get on and do it themselves really. Children in the class would be asking questions about things that perhaps they would be expecting an answer to. So, for example, 'I've finished this, I don't know what to do now', and then my standard answer would be, 'Well, what do you think you should do?' rather than 'Go and do that'.

Daniel: My role as a teacher is to try and make the children independent learners. It's giving them the skills so they'd be able to go do their own work and learn and develop. So I think, for a primary school teacher, the main sort of focus is to give them basic skills so that later in life, they can use those skills in order to do their own research and learn by themselves.

What is your understanding of learning?

Daniel: I think there are *two* views of learning. One I would probably say is subject knowledge, learning the content, learning different bits, and I think that's why some people can be classed as intelligent, as 'have a good memory', because they can remember that subject knowledge. I think the other side of learning is the ability to learn by yourself, make mistakes, learn from those mistakes – the process of how you get to a final answer. I think you can be good at either, but I think to actually learn you need to have both. You need to have subject knowledge but also the ability to understand what you are being taught, to be able to find out by yourself, and to maybe make it applicable to you in your life. I think that's the key bit, making it meaningful, because that inspires you to learn or makes it relevant.

Judith: Some children in our class learn better working together in pairs or in groups. Other children respond better to more verbal work, where they can do lots of talking. Others are happy to sit and listen, to be told what to do and they go straight on and do it. I think our class, particularly, learn from 'hands on'. They like being involved in things; they like the doing, they like the practical things. And they learn from each other. I think they're quite happy to take ideas from each other; use them. And I think that's a help in their learning.

Discussion point

a. How do you think the views expressed by these teachers correspond to or differ from the theories of learning outlined in this chapter? Remember that Bruner wrote about scaffolding learning, the spiral curriculum and learning as culture; Marton and Booth talked about learning as experience and distinguished between surface learning and deep learning; and Wenger used the phrase 'communities of practice' to focus attention on social aspects of learning, especially 'participation' and 'identity'.

Pupils' perspectives on the nature of learning

When it comes down to it, however, it is not just the adults in the school who define what learning actually is, and therefore how to motivate pupils to learn – it is the pupils themselves who, consciously or otherwise, perceive and experience learning and who will determine what motivates them.

Here is part of a conversation held between two girls who are in a year 4 class in a junior school. They both hold positive attitudes towards school and learning:

Pupils have their say

Dawn: If you are a good learner you always listen. You're always focused on the teacher. Stuff like that.

Linda: And you're not confused, because if you *are* confused you'll probably go to the teacher and if you *don't* and then you're just like stuck and confused.

Dawn: But you can be a good learner and still be confused, can't you?

Linda: Yes you can.

Dawn: I think we are both good learners because we've made lots of progress.

Linda: I think learning is easy for me because the *teacher* explains it. Learning is like if you don't know something, and then you find out about something about that thing; for example, when I was little I didn't know about sharks, and now I do because we're doing habitats and stuff.

Discussion points

a. To what extent do you think the views expressed by these two pupils are typical of what pupils think about learning?

b. In what ways do you think that they correspond to, or differ from, the learning theories discussed in this chapter? For example, how do you think they relate to Wenger's concept of communities of practice or Marton and Booth's distinction between surface and deep learning?

c. Given what these pupils said, how would you expect them to be motivated to learn?

Theories of childhood

> The wind cried and sobbed like a child in the chimney.
>
> (Arthur Conan Doyle, *The Adventures of Sherlock Holmes*)

Motivating children to learn requires that we not only think about what it means to learn, but also what it means to be a child. And just as our understanding of learning is gained from the views held within our society and culture, so how we think about what a child is can also be gathered from those around us.

What's wrong with sending a boy up a chimney or down a mine? Why shouldn't a ten-year-old girl sew and stitch into the small hours or spend her nights scouring the rubbish dump for something to hawk in the morning? Each and every child in this situation will learn 'stuff' necessary to live. They will therefore be receiving an education of sorts. Of course, no one would (or should) agree that these are acceptable ways to treat children, yet we do need to appreciate that our western, modern concept of childhood is as culturally constructed as the concept of education itself, and the two concepts are intimately linked.

Much of our views regarding the purposes of education relate to what we mean by the term 'child' – and, like 'schooling' itself, this is not something to be taken for granted. The concept of 'childhood' has changed through the centuries and changes across cultures and societies even today. The long summer holidays in Britain hark back to the time when concessions were made in the process of bringing in compulsory education for all children. Children were given weeks off school not to relax and go on holiday, but to work in the fields and help bring in the harvest.

What is a child?

Through the centuries and across cultures, the following views have been held and, to some extent, continue to be held today – always, it is worth noting, held by adults about what children are or should be.

- 'Children should be seen and not heard.'

Children do not have individuality or personage in their own right. They are simply 'there'. They are to be cared for and looked after, but they do not have meaning until they become adults and take up responsibilities within their society. Children are largely empty vessels into which knowledge and instruction can be poured.

- 'Mini' adult.

The only difference between adults and children is their size. Everything that pertains to an adult pertains to the child. As soon as they are physically capable, they go to work supporting their family. Their role in life is simply to grow up, become adults themselves and reproduce after their own kind, in order to maintain the survival of the family.

- Insurance for old age.

Children are there to look after their parents in the event of their illness or when they become old and can no longer look after themselves. By that time the children are likely to have become adults, and to have had children of their own, but, nevertheless, the expectation is that they will look after their aged parents and relatives. The more children an adult has, the more chance they have of being looked after properly.

Impact on education

Arguably, in its history, much of formal education in Britain has been along the lines of the first view of childhood: children are empty vessels to be filled with knowledge from those who know more and know better than they do. The classroom was a place in which children sat quietly, listening to and taking in what was being told to them. There was no place for discovery or exploration. This is not the case today.

Links between how 'childhood' is viewed or defined and how we teach

In what has come to be known as the 'new sociology of childhood', children are not passive recipients of something done to them by others (parents, teachers, etc.), nor are they simply persons marking time or being prepared for the 'real' life of adulthood. Rather, children are considered to be active participants in their growth and learning which results in the creation of their own understandings, experiences and cultures. As in Bruner's theory of learning, children actively 'make meanings' for themselves out of their learning; they do not simply accept and take in what is being handed down to them. Children are still obviously bio-logically more immature than adults, and remain children, but they are individuals and communities in their own right, an already existing part of society.

Christensen and Prout (2005) use the phrase 'webs of significance' (p. 50) when seeking to investigate the complex interaction of relationships experienced by children within school and outside of it. This phrase is a particularly helpful one when seeking to investigate the interplay between children, motivation and their experience of schooling. Children do not experience single lines of communication or relationships: their lives are more like a spider's web of interlocking and intersecting connections with other people and with a range of environments. The classroom is not a single, simple entity; it is rather a 'web of significance', as is the playground, the school as a whole and the child's home. In each of these situations children relate to different adults (teachers, teaching assistants, head teachers, parents, carers, babysitters, aunts, uncles, grandparents) and to different children (brothers and sisters, cousins, friends, acquaintances, enemies).

Each one of these relationships helps shape how children feel about themselves and view themselves as learners, and each one will have an impact on their motivation to learn in school. However, not all of these strands of the 'webs of significance' will hold the *same* significance for each child. The family is probably the most significant of these webs, with the school probably coming a close second in terms of its influence in shaping the child's perception of who and what they are as learners. To complicate things even further, children respond to this shaping in a range of ways – there is no set pattern or predictable outcome. Children do not create their own meaning of life in a vacuum; it is done through the interplay of their own personalities, personal experiences and the adult world around them. It is also done in conjunction with other children. In the technological world in which we live, children are now more and more influenced by mass media and the internet, particularly social networking sites.

This point of view of childhood has enormous implications for education.

Case study 1.8: Miss Pitcher's class

Miss Pitcher is taking her year 6 class for literacy. They are in the midst of a series of lessons aimed at giving the children the opportunity to write an extended narrative. Over the course of two weeks the story has developed from a simple plan to a more complex pattern whereby different characters, plots and sub-plots have been intro-duced. Today, she is asking the class to write some notes about their thoughts to do with how a dilemma confronting the central character could be resolved.

She instructs the class to write key words only on their planning sheet – 'Just notes, not big sentences'. She then says, 'Nobody can do that for you – it's all your own thoughts and feelings about the dilemma.' After ten minutes, she tells the class to stop work and, if they are happy with their work and it is completed to give it to her, otherwise put it in their trays to be completed later in the day.

Their next activity involves splitting into groups to discuss how the plot might develop. Several of the class ask to go to the library to change their books, to which Miss agrees. As they are going out, two boys get into a fight right outside the classroom door. Miss goes outside to try to sort it out and is gone five minutes. One of the boys, in particular, is very upset and distressed. During this time, more pupils go to the library, this time without asking permission from the teacher. They take advantage of Miss Pitcher not being in the room to supervise them. At one time, only nine pupils are left in the classroom.

When Miss Pitcher does come back into the classroom, she praises the pupils who helped by ignoring the fight and staying in their places, continuing with their work rather than taking themselves off to the library. She then talks with the class about what the rest should have done in the situation. She asks the class to think about what each of them did to make the class better – 'Who thinks they *did* help?' – and waits for children to put up their hands.

On another occasion, Miss Pitcher aims to provide opportunities for her class to reflect on their progress in literacy. She distributes to the pupils the exercise books in which they have written literacy assessments over the past year. She asks the class to look back through their books and see how they have improved since their last assessment. She then asks them to say how their work on their stories has helped them in their assessment. She asks the children to show their work to the person they are sitting next to, so that they can comment on each other's work. Miss Pitcher then chooses a text written by one of her most able writers and reads it aloud to the class as a model of what could be written. She asks the class to put their hands up if they want to say anything about the writing. She continues: 'Two minutes to talk with each other if you can't think of anything by yourself. Talk with each other.' Then she asks for comments from the children.

Discussion points

a. What do you think this case study tell us about Miss Pitcher's view of teaching?
b. What do you think it tells us about her views of children?
c. What choices and responsibilities was she encouraging in the pupils in her class?

What pupils say about the purpose of school

'Student or pupil voice' is an often-heard phrase in today's schools, but it can mean different things to different people. *How* the views and opinions of pupils are gathered is crucial to an understanding of 'pupil voice'. Listening to what pupils have to say follows the principles of the 'new sociology of childhood', which seeks to recognise children as being active participants in their own learning and, in Bruner's terminology, as being 'meaning makers' in their own right.

Here, several children discuss what they think they go to school for. Their ages range from nine to eleven.

What the pupils say

Matthew: I enjoy learning. I know going to school and learning will lead to something good further on in my life. You need qualifications for the job you want.

Nathan: That's true – so I can get a really good job and have lots of money.

Philip: 'Cos nearly every job involves what you do at school.

Eric: If we didn't do school we wouldn't learn to do anything so we wouldn't be able to do any jobs.

Andrew: But in school you meet new friends and learn from them.

Benjamin: Yes, it's getting together and learning.

Sarah: I enjoy coming to school 'cos I get to see my friends. It's really the only time I get to see them – at school.

Joan: Friends can share each other's ideas. But sometimes we talk as well.

Sarah: Sometimes I think, wouldn't it be great if we could just transplant all this that you learnt into your brain so that you instantly know it. But then it's not the same.

Benjamin: You wouldn't be *learning* anything.

Peter: I'm alright at school. I know that school is a means of education, but it's like, when your parents are at work it's like a caring unit, if you get what I mean. Like a place you'd go while your parents are at work, but learning at the same time.

Adele: I get forced to go to school.

Discussion points

a.   How do these views compare with the views of pupils you know and teach?

b.   How do you feel about the comments made by these pupils?

c.   What further things would you like them to have said?

d.   What would you have liked to ask them?

Summary

In this chapter, we have looked at:

- Some of the reasons why schools might exist – the purposes of education – and have seen that the purpose of education is more complex than it seems and is determined by many factors, including what is important to society at the time.
- Various theories about learning – what is meant by 'learning' – and have discovered that there is not one single view of learning but rather many, some focusing on individual children's development of thinking ('brain power'), others concentrating more on how children learn together in a social environment.
- How these various theories of learning and purposes of education might impact on pupil motivation – acknowledging that pupils have to be motivated towards some sort of goal.
- Several teachers' views and opinions about learning, about their roles and about how and why children respond differently to similar teaching strategies.

- Various theories of what it means to be a child, to experience 'childhood' and have seen that, like 'education', 'childhood' is largely defined by what society values and deems to be important.
- How children's self-identity as learners can be developed, primarily looking at the influence of the school.
- Some pupils' reasons for going to school and saw that future prospects were an important part of their thinking and motivation, even at a young age.

Chapter 2

Motivation – the theories

An overview

This chapter begins with a story.

Somewhere Secondary School

Josie, the learning support assistant (LSA), sat in a science class with the three students whom she was supporting and encouraging to complete a worksheet on aspects of the periodic table. They worked on the task, but Josie felt that their enthusiasm was somewhat lacking to say the least, despite the fact that they had all built a good relationship with her. Anwar summed it up when he said: 'As if I am ever going to use this.'

Meanwhile, the din from the rest of the class grew louder and louder as the teacher, Ms Smythe, tried to engage the class in a revision task to a chorus of 'What's the point? I am never going to need this!'. . . 'It's boring!' . . . 'I can't do science and never will'. However, to be fair, there were a few students who were working on the revision task, their heads down, reading and writing despite the increasing noise around them.

As the noise grew, the comments grew increasingly disrespectful, with one student loudly swearing at Ms Smythe. Ms Smythe swiftly sent the rude pupil out of the classroom to stand in the corridor.

Thankfully, the lesson finally ended and Josie and Ms Smythe managed to have a two to three minute chat on aspects of the lesson before they had to dash to separate classrooms. Josie reported that her students had finished their worksheets. Although Anwar needed more support than Brooklyn, perhaps both would benefit from further revision. Josie and Ms Smythe agreed that, all in all, the lesson had gone fairly well.

However, privately, Josie thought:

> Ms Smythe needs to be stricter. She needs to show them who's the boss. I wish I could step in and tell that lot just what I think of them. I hate it when they are disrespectful to her, but I don't want to offend Ms Smythe and it is not my place to tell her what to do. She is the teacher. But who can blame them for not being interested – chemistry is so boring! And that revision exercise! I know Ms Smythe said she tried to make it fun, but is that what she thinks is fun? Maybe she should give prizes – chocolate bars – that would engage them.

Meanwhile, privately, Ms Smythe thought:

> I know that Josie thinks that she could handle the class better than me but she just doesn't understand. I know that Josie thinks I should yell and scream but she just

doesn't appreciate the background that some of these pupils come from. The fact that they are here and have opened a book is a real achievement. I suppose I should try to make it more fun – but there are times that I feel that I am here to entertain and not to teach. Whatever happened to the joy of learning? Of course, other teachers give prizes and stickers, but when I was their age I wanted to learn. I wanted to find out about things: I was curious. I couldn't read enough. And as for prizes! If they think they are going to get a chocolate bar for every right answer, well that's not going to happen in the real world. They have to find the motivation within themselves!

Making sense of the story

After reading the story you may be thinking – yes, that is my class – or you may think that you have never experienced a class like that. However, what the story does illustrate is the complexity of motivation and how motivation is linked to both learning and behaviour. Indeed the story raises more questions than answers.

How would you analyse what is happening within that imaginary class?

Perhaps, to analyse the situation, it is first helpful to look at the class from the perspective of the pupils.

You could say that the pupils responded to the task in a number of ways. Some pupils were apathetic – they felt there was no point and they seemed to have no motivation for the task in hand – while a few pupils were actively engaged. Using the relevant terminology, the pupils who were apathetic (that is, who felt there was no point) are said to have *amotivation*. Those who were actively engaged despite all the noise around them could be referred to as having *intrinsic motivation*. Intrinsic motivation involves engaging in an activity for its own sake. An individual who is intrinsically motivated will experience a sense of personal satisfaction and pleasure from engaging in that activity. This view of motivation sees motivation as stemming from within; it is part of an individual's personality – that is, something which the pupil brings to the learning situation.

However, other theorists would argue that those involved in teaching and supporting learning can have an important impact on motivation of the pupils. *Demotivation* refers to aspects of the classroom environment or the learning situation that can cancel out even strong existing motivation in pupils (Dornyei 2001, p. 3). Perhaps, in the story, the manner in which the lesson was presented had a negative impact on the pupils' motivation to engage in learning. As Josie stated, what the pupils needed was fun – perhaps prizes as suggested. Those pupils whose behaviour is driven by a 'what's in it for me' attitude are said to be *extrinsically motivated*; that is, the source of their motivation lies outside themselves. However, as the teacher, Ms Smythe, pointed out, the pupils are not going to receive a chocolate bar for every correct answer when they leave school and they therefore need to be intrinsically motivated to achieve in the real world.

But how can you tell if a student is motivated? Well, on one level you could say if pupils are engaged in the learning task then they must be motivated. But what is the source of their motivation? Consider the few pupils who were engaged; a teacher/teaching assistant might assume that they were intrinsically motivated. But are there other explanations? Possibly, the pupils' parents have offered them substantial amounts of money for every good pass at GCSE. Possibly the pupils are terrified of not doing their work and facing a school detention, or perhaps they actually have a passion for chemistry. Likewise, what motivates those pupils who do not engage in the leaning task? It could be that pupils are very motivated by many things, but not what is being presented in the classroom situation. And, of course, there will be differences between pupils who could do the task if they wanted to and pupils who can't do the task as they lack the necessary ability. But, again, how can you tell what motivates individual pupils? It seems that you need to actually find out what is going on within pupils' minds. What are they thinking? What are the pupils saying to themselves about the tasks? It is important to talk to pupils about what they find motivating.

On another level, what is the role of the teacher and teaching assistant in influencing motivation? In discussing motivation it is easy to focus on the individual, but factors outside the individual have a role to play. In the imaginary story, Ms Smythe mentioned the impact of the home environment and, of course, family background is important, as are the influences of peers and the culture of the school. Dornyei (2001) sees the role of those involved in teaching as one of directing and energising activities within the classroom. Teaching professionals are designated leaders. They 'embody group conscience, symbolise the group's unity and identity, and serve as a model or a reference/standard' (Dornyei 2001, p. 35). This view places much emphasis on the teacher and teaching assistant. Here, we see that the enthusiasm and attitudes of the teacher and teaching assistant are all important. Enthusiasm is contagious.

Of course, you could say that the imaginary story is just a very brief snapshot of the class in question and of course you would be right. Perhaps the behaviour is not typical and that it was last period on a Friday afternoon. But this addresses another important issue regarding how motivation can change with time. Within any lesson and within the course of the school year, energies and the motivation to engage and sustain activity will ebb and flow. From an individual perspective, motivation not only encompasses the initial decision to choose an activity, but also the willingness to persevere with the activity, perhaps over an extended period of time.

On a final point, it is important to consider the role of the teacher and the teaching assistant in motivating each other and the impact that their relationship has on pupil outcomes, specifically pupil learning, behaviour and motivation. What was apparent in the imaginary story was that, although both Ms Smythe (teacher) and Josie (LSA) agreed that the lesson had gone fairly well, there was much between them that was left unsaid. The question remains as to whether planning for future classes could be enhanced by a more honest and constructive dialogue between the teacher and teaching assistant. Implications of the teacher/teaching assistant relationship will be discussed in greater detail in Chapter 3.

To recap: in order to analyse a situation in terms of motivational issues, it is helpful to:

- Look at the situation from the pupils' perspective.
- Consider both personality and environmental factors (for example, individual, class-room, school, family, peers, etc.).
- Be aware that there are different types of motivation, for example intrinsic and extrinsic.
- Discuss with pupils what they find motivating and what motivates them.
- Consider your role in directing and energising the motivation levels within the class-room, including your relationships with fellow staff.
- Encourage pupils to take responsibility for their own motivation.

What this story has provided is an introduction to issues of motivation and, as stated previously, the story raises more questions than answers. Table 2.1 lists questions about motivation – perhaps you have more.

Table 2.1 'What I have always wanted to know about motivation'

How do pupils become intrinsically motivated?

Is intrinsic motivation the optimal form or the 'holy grail' of motivation?

How can those involved in the teaching profession encourage the development of intrinsic motivation?

Does the way that pupils think about motivation change with age?

Does offering rewards diminish intrinsic motivation?

Is there a place for rewards and sanctions in the classroom?

How can a teacher/teaching assistant direct and energise the motivational levels of pupils in his or her classroom?

How can a teacher/teaching assistant sustain positive levels of motivation within him or herself, and within the pupils, over time?

How does the role of the family and society in general impact on motivation?

Having introduced a number of concepts regarding motivation and even more questions, we turn to a discussion of relevant definitions and theories in pursuit of both answers and practical ways forward.

Definitions

Motivation is one of those words that we use often and in many different contexts but which proves somewhat elusive to define.

In everyday terms, motivation could be defined as 'get up and go'. When someone loses their motivation we could say that their 'get up and go has got up and gone'.

A classic theory of motivation described by Hull (1943) saw motivation as a drive; that is, a source of energy for individual behaviour. Hull stated that whereas learning involved the direction or focus of the behaviour, motivation encompassed the intensity and duration of said behaviour. So, for example, a pupil may be focused or directed by the teacher to learn maths, but pupil motivation to learn would involve how long (duration) and how hard (intensity) they applied themselves to the task.

Dornyei (2001) describes motivation as involving the choice of, persistence with and effort expended on an activity. He (p. 8) states that motivation can account for:

• Why people decide to do something.
• How long they are willing to sustain the activity.
• How hard they are going to pursue it.

All of these questions are central in supporting pupil learning!

The theories of motivation

Achievement motivation: nothing ventured nothing gained, or nothing ventured nothing lost

Atkinson (1964) offered a theory on achievement motivation which was very influential at the time and still has relevance to educational practitioners today. He believed that motivation to achieve was a personality characteristic and that individuals differed on the degree to which they viewed success or failure as important. Those individuals who were success-orientated experienced an inner sense of pride and other positive emotions both when they experienced success and when they anticipated they would succeed. Of course, the degree to which individuals would experience these positive emotions would vary from individual to individual. The source of these positive emotions was internal; that is, intrinsic and not dependent on external sources such as praise from parents, peers or teachers. The theory became more complex when Atkinson noted that some successes were more important than others. Those successes that were difficult to achieve were valued more and generated more positive emotions than those successes that were perceived as easy; that is, when anyone could do them. Atkinson predicted that a motivation to succeed would lead individuals to choose tasks of an intermediate difficulty level – tasks that were challenging but 'doable'. Further, Atkinson predicted that those with a relatively high level of achievement motivation would monitor their own responses and move on to more challenging tasks when they succeeded, and backtrack to slightly easier tasks when they experienced difficulty. These pupils believed 'nothing ventured, nothing gained'.

However, central to Atkinson's theory is that the motive to avoid failure can be as great as the motive to achieve. Just as those who are achievement-orientated experience positive emotions from achieving, those who have a strong motive to avoid failure experience strong negative emotions, such as anxiety, when they fail – and, likewise, a strong feeling of anxiety from just thinking about failing. This, Atkinson believed, leads pupils to choose tasks that are really easy to achieve (where there is no chance of failure) or, on the other hand, tasks that are so difficult that no one could achieve them. Atkinson argues that with very difficult or almost impossible tasks, the consequence of failing is not perceived as threatening as almost everyone would fail. Though these choices do not lead to effective learning, they do protect the individual pupil's self-esteem from potentially damaging consequences of failure. These pupils are best characterised by the phrase 'nothing ventured, nothing lost'. Atkinson believed that, for pupils who had a high motive to avoid failure, classroom systems of rewards or sanctions could be used to encourage pupils to engage and persevere with tasks (Galloway et al. 1998).

How can the theory of achievement motivation be applied to the classroom?

First and foremost, this theory tells us that pupils will differ in the type of motivation they experience (whether they are motivated to succeed or motivated to avoid failure) and the degree to which the type of motivation influences their behaviour; that is, whether or not they have a strong drive to achieve or a moderate drive. Knowing what motivation is driving pupils can help teachers and teaching assistants plan the way in which they support pupils.

Case study 2.1: Trying to measure motivation

John was interested in measuring the motivation of pupils in his classroom. He gave his year 6 pupils a questionnaire in which he simply asked:

How important is it to you to succeed?

1	*2*	*3*
Very important	*Slightly important*	*Not bothered*

How important is it to you to avoid failure?

1	*2*	*3*
Very important	*Slightly important*	*Not bothered*

John reported that he found the results both surprising and revealing.

Discussion points

a. Do you think this is a fair way of measuring achievement motivation?
b. How else could you gather pupils' attitudes to success and failure?

From the perspective of the classroom, the ideal pupil is a pupil who is intrinsically motivated and success-orientated – in terms of wanting to achieve success in the subject area that is being taught – and who monitors his or her own performance. This pupil would more likely to engage in 'deep learning' and to see learning as a way of changing oneself (see pp. 14–15). This pupil is an independent learner; however, most pupils need support and guidance to develop these skills.

How do pupils come to have a high motive to succeed and how can teachers and teaching assistants influence this? Atkinson argues that the motivation to engage or succeed is, in part, determined by the value of the task as perceived by the pupil. For those pupils who cannot see for themselves the value of the task, then the role of the teacher/teaching assistant can be to highlight this aspect.

Though Atkinson saw achievement motivation as a personality characteristic, this theory stresses the importance of how pupils' inner-thinking and feelings influence their behaviour in the classroom. One way forward would have teachers and teaching assistants engaging pupils in talking about issues of motivation. Such conversations would allow teachers and teaching assistants to both encourage positive attitudes and to challenge and work through negative ones.

Expectancy-value theories

Atkinson's (1964, 1974) work on achievement motivation has been developed and expanded in a more general set of theories now known as 'expectancy-value'. One group of theories focus on a pupil's expectation of success, that is, whether they believe that they can do a task, while another group of theories focus on the value of the task; that is, whether they want to do it.

When a pupil considers whether they can do a task, theorists and researchers now believe that a pupil (Dornyei 2001):

- Actively focuses on his or her past experiences when they are thinking about and explaining past successes and failures. These theories are known as attribution theories.
- Makes judgments on his or her own ability and competence in undertaking the task. These theories concern self-efficacy.
- Examines the cost or benefit of engaging in the task in terms of the impact on their self-esteem. These theories are known as self-worth theories.

To recap, pupils ask themselves questions, such as: What happened last time I tried this? Why did it happen? What does this tell me about my competence or ability? What does it mean to me if I try? What does it mean to me if I try and succeed? What does it mean to me if I try and fail?

Attribution theories

Weiner (1986, 1992) stressed the cognitive aspect; he believed individuals reflect, analyse and make judgments on past successes and failures. This analysis and judgment influences an individual's future expectation of success or failure – which in turn influences his or her motivation to engage in a task.

Weiner (1986) believed that causal attributions – that is, how an individual interprets success or failure – can be in two dimensions:

internal v. external causes and *stable v. unstable causes*

Graham (1994) cites ability, effort, task difficulty, luck, mood, family background and help and hindrance from others as common explanations that pupils give to explain their successes and failure, with most explanations focusing on ability and effort. In Weiner's original model he made a distinction between ability and effort, but this was revised in later versions. Weiner felt it was more appropriate to talk of aptitude rather than ability, as aptitude was felt to signal a more enduring and internal characteristic, and there was a need to further differentiate between degrees of effort (Schunk et al. 2010).

Table 2.2 Locus of causality

	Internal cause	*External cause*
Stable cause	Aptitude Long-term effort	Objective task characteristics, such as task difficulty
Unstable cause	Temporary or situational effort	Chance

(Source: Weiner 1986. Diagram adapted from Schunk et al. 2010, p. 99)

Although this theory is complex, a key insight is that individuals differ in their personal interpretations as to what causes success or failure. Interpretations matter, as pupils' beliefs will influence their future behaviours; that is, their motivation to engage in learning. In Table 2.3 we will see that some interpretations or outlooks are considered more optimal for future learning than others. Consider the following, in which both Joe and Hayley have achieved a grade B on their maths tests.

What is of real interest in this example is that, although both pupils received the same grade, how they explained their successes differed.

In terms of the theory, those pupils who expect to be successful in the future attribute:

- successes to internal and stable causes (I have a flair and I consistently work hard); and
- failures to external and stable causes (the test was not fair) or internal and unstable causes (I didn't try but next time I will). It is worth noting that failure is *not* seen as a personal reflection on aptitude or ability and that self-esteem is protected.

As a result of this more optimistic attitude, the motivation for these pupils to engage in future tasks is higher, and this frame of thinking is associated with high achievement. It would seem, therefore, that this way of thinking should be encouraged.

On the other hand, those pupils who do not have expectations that they will be successful in the future:

- attribute successes to external unstable factors (such as chance, e.g. 'It was my lucky day'); and
- failures to internal and stable factors ('I am useless').

Table 2.3 Interpretations matter – explanations Joe and Hayley have given about achieving grade B in maths

Joe			Hayley		
	Internal	**External**		**Internal**	**External**
Stable	I have a flair for maths but I have also worked consistently hard this year and I have always handed in my homework.	The test was fair.	**Stable**	I am useless at maths.	The test was hard.
Unstable	Yes I revised for the test, but the key to my success was the fact that I continually worked at trying to understand the subject.	Luck played no part in my grade.	**Unstable**	I did study very hard, but only the night before as my mother was going on at me.	I was very lucky. The teacher must have been in a really good mood.

The result of this pessimistic outlook on future success prospects is that the motivation to engage in future tasks is lower and, therefore, typically this frame of thinking is associated with lower achievement.

But let's return to our example. Joe's frame of thinking regarding having a certain amount of flair, valuing effort, and his behaviour in consistently working hard would seem to predict that Joe is going places. However, Hayley's thinking is hard to understand. She only studied when nagged by her mother. Yet, despite believing that she was useless at maths, Hayley achieved a high grade. Hayley's achievement indicates that she has great potential to do well in the subject, but that her frame of thinking could hold her back.

How attribution theory can be applied to the classroom: attribution retraining

What attribution theory has taught those involved in education is that there is an important distinction between the outcome of the task (in terms of mark or grade awarded) and the individual pupil's interpretation of the outcome ('why did I receive the mark I did?'). Consequently, much thought has focused on what has been termed as attribution retraining; that is, to make the pupil aware and conscious of how he or she thinks and how to adopt more positive ways of thinking. The assumption is that changing ways of thinking leads to changes in behaviour. Therefore, if a pupil thinks positively about learning challenges, then they are more likely to be motivated to engage in learning. Obviously, teacher/teaching assistant feedback is crucial in changing pupils' attitudes to learning.

Classic research in this area (Dweck 1975) involved presenting pupils who had become 'helpless' in the face of repeated failures in maths with two types of possible interventions. One group of helpless pupils received training with problems that were guaranteed to result in success; the tasks set were selected according to individual ability so that they were achievable for the pupils. The argument behind this was that the positive experience of being successful would be rewarding to the pupils and consequently they would change their attitudes to engaging with maths problems. The other training group received a mix of problems, some guaranteed to result in success but others made impossible to solve so that the pupils would deliberately experience failure. When the pupils experienced failure the teacher would say that they did not try hard enough. This strategy was based on the view that renewed effort in the face of challenge is crucial to learning.

Surprisingly, the results of this study showed that the pupils who had received maths problems that were all achievable later fell apart or gave up when they experienced failure, whereas the pupils who had experienced impossible maths problems and had been told to try harder later persisted in challenging learning situations in which they had initially experienced failure.

Subsequent research (Chapin and Dyck 1976; Relich et al. 1986) showed that teaching pupils to explain learning failures in terms of lack of effort had a positive impact on future achievement.

One insight to be gained from this area of research is that an important aspect of learning is learning how to deal with failure. Many teachers and teaching assistants can describe very able pupils who simply fall apart when things get difficult. An important application would have teachers and teaching assistants acting as role models in demonstrating positive responses to both success and failure situations, in order to help develop pupils' adaptive responses.

Case study 2.2: Developing positive attitudes to learning challenges

Leon is a very able pupil and very rarely, that is almost never fails or gets any question wrong.

Leon: I can't believe it – I have got two maths questions wrong. There must be a mistake.

Mr T: Look at the problem again . . ..

Leon: I am not going to do this.

Mr T: Leon, I don't like making mistakes either, but sometimes everybody makes mistakes.

Leon: I can't even look at the problem.

Mr T: When I make a mistake – and I do make mistakes – I take some deep breaths and tell myself that I can learn more from my mistakes than my successes. Sometimes I need to repeat this several times to myself. Then I go back to the problem.

Leon (tearfully): Ok – what did you say to yourself?

Case study 2.3: From unhealthy to healthy attributions

Programmes that enhance healthy (internal and controllable) attributions or effort attributions are recommended to increase pupils' motivation to learn and help pupils take responsibility for their learning. With this in mind, Donna decided to investigate her pupils' attributions. She designed a questionnaire measuring attribution which she asked her class to complete. For each question there was one answer that indicated ability attributions, one answer than indicated effort attributions and one answer that indicated external attributions.

One example of an attribution question was as follows:

Suppose you received the highest grade on the class science test. This is probably because:

	False	Mostly False	Sometimes False, Sometimes True	Mostly True	True
a. You are the best at science.	❑	❑	❑	❑	❑
b. You always try hard in science classes.	❑	❑	❑	❑	❑
c. It was your lucky day.	❑	❑	❑	❑	❑

(In terms of scoring: *question a,* indicates attitudes towards ability; *question b,* indicates attitudes towards effort and *question c,* indicates attitudes to external factors.)

On analysing her results, Donna discovered that she had a number of children who had *unhealthy attributions*. One type of unhealthy attribution involved having low effort attributions; that is, these pupils did not seem to think their effort made a difference. Another type of *unhealthy attribution* was making external attributions. These pupils would attribute successes to external factors that were not in their control. For example, the reason they scored a goal was that the wind had blown the ball into the net or the reason they had received a good mark was that it was their lucky day. For these children, Donna implemented an attribution retraining programme that had been developed through the local education psychology service.

As Donna stated:

> The attribution retraining programme involved the children participating in a number of activities. One activity required pupils to brainstorm why they thought people succeeded or failed and this was used to make them aware of a range of possible explanations. To stress the impact of practice on learning, a series of fun memory games were used. For example, the pupils were asked to first memorise a list of words. As a group we recorded how we did and then I taught them various strategies for improving memory. When we tried the same game again, all the pupils improved their scores. The lesson of the memory game was that effort and the use of strategies can make a difference. The next activity we worked on was 'self-talk'; that is, what pupils say to themselves when they face a challenging task. To do this, I would work individually with the pupils on challenging tasks getting them to verbalise what they were thinking and encouraging them to use positive self-statements.

> Did this programme work? Well, the pupils do seem to be taking more responsibility for their successes, which promotes self-esteem and motivates them to engage in similar challenges in the future. And in response to situations in which they get a question wrong or get stuck or think that they will fail they are now more likely to use positive self-statements and have a go. They are more likely to say things like: 'I made a silly mistake – which I can fix' or 'I didn't understand it properly and I need more practice and I need to ask for help.' So, on the whole, the programme worked, though it worked for some pupils more than others.

> (Based on the work of Scott 2011)

Discussion points

a. What activities do you use that:
    i.   Encourage pupils to think about success and failure;
    ii. Help pupils to examine what they say to themselves when faced with a challenging situation;
    iii. Demonstrate to pupils that practice and strategy use can enhance learning?

Table 2.4 Type of feedback statements

Feedback statement	What does it do?
You have worked hard.	Links effort with past achievements.
You will need to work hard.	Links effort with future achievements.
You are good at this.	Acknowledges ability.
You are good at this because you have worked hard.	Acknowledges the link between past effort and ability.
You can be good at this but you need to work hard.	Acknowledges the link between effort and potential ability.
You have tried hard but you need to try a different approach. I suggest that you try this approach . . .	Acknowledges effort but suggests a change in strategy is needed if success is to be achieved.

In terms of more recent research in this area, the focus has shifted to the specific type of feedback, whether ability or effort feedback is more influential and whether something additional is needed.

Early work in this field, such as Dweck (1975), focused on saying statements such as 'try harder' and, although this may be effective with some pupils, those involved in teaching can probably recall situations in which pupils have really tried and still have failed. Clearly, just saying 'try harder' to those pupils would not be useful and can be demotivating. What is essential in terms of feedback is that feedback should be perceived as honest, authentic and credible by the pupil. Feedback also needs to be specific, detailed and constructive, as it needs to inform the pupil of what they have done and what they need to do next (see p. 122 for further discussion).

Developmental changes in thinking about ability and effort

What attribution theory and attribution retraining research has highlighted is the complex relationship between ability and effort. Nicholls (1990) believed that our understanding of how ability and effort is related develops with age, and that a young child's understanding is not the same as that of an adult. The stages are shown in Table 2.5.

Discussion points

Joe spends a lot of time studying, revising and doing homework. When an exam is coming up, Joe will turn down opportunities to go out with his friends in order to study. Joe is a straight A pupil.

Callum is a party animal. Callum listens in class but spends little time on homework or studying. When an exam is coming up, Callum's social life always comes first. Callum is also a straight A pupil.

a.   Who is the most able, and why?
b.   Who is most likely to achieve their potential, and why?

Table 2.5 How beliefs regarding the relationship between ability and effort develop

Age	Beliefs	Examples of what they believe
3 to 5 years	Effort or outcome is ability.	Children who try harder are smarter. Children who get the best marks try the hardest and are smarter.
6 to 8 years	Effort is the cause of outcomes.	Children who try equally hard should receive the same result (outcome) regardless of ability.
9 to 10 years	Effort and ability are partially differentiated.	Children who try equally hard may not always get the same result (outcome).
12 to 13 years	Ability is capacity.	Ability and effort are separate factors. Ability has a set capacity and this capacity level influences the impact that effort can have. If ability level is low, no matter how much effort is applied there is a limit on how much can be achieved (the outcome). If two pupils achieve the same result (the outcome is equal), then lower effort implies higher ability.

(Nicholls (1990). Table adapted from Schunk et al. 2010, p. 111.)

Nicholls (1990) further states that the view that ability is capacity is a view that most adults hold in western societies. The consequence of this view is that most adults believe that if you have to work hard at a task you have less ability, and that if you have high ability then you will *not* need to work as hard in order to achieve. Most adults would believe that effort can and does make a difference, but that the impact of effort is limited. Therefore, ability or aptitude is seen as a stable and unchanging personal quality. However, there has been much recent debate regarding the views or *mindsets* of individuals as regards the relationship between ability and effort, and we will discuss in a later section (see pp. 58–60).

The implications of this theory in terms of teacher/teaching assistant feedback is that comments stressing effort are effective in the early years while feedback linking ability and effort with effective strategy use is more effective with older children/pupils.

Self-worth theory

Covington (1992) believed that pupils' perception of ability was important as it impacted on their sense of self-worth. Covington's 'self-worth' theory sees the pursuit of self-acceptance as being of the highest priority, and that in school self-acceptance depends on achievement – thus 'school achievement is best understood in terms of attempts by students to maintain a positive self-image of competency, particularly when risking competitive failure' (p. 74).

If self-worth is defined by academic achievement, then academic failure comes at a high price. Covington states that this can lead to a number of behaviours:

• Pupils may lie about the amount of effort they have put into a task so that others will think that their successes are due to ability alone. For example, pupils may say: 'I didn't try at all', when in fact they did try.

- Pupils may exhibit self-handicapping behaviour; that is, they may purposefully not study for an exam or study at the last minute so that, if they do not do as well as they hoped, they can explain this by the fact that they did not try. This strategy may preserve self-worth, but it can lead to underachievement.

From a pupil's perspective, it seems that the worst thing that can happen is to really try and to fail. However, what would be worse still is to have others know that you really tried but still couldn't do it. In order to prevent self-handicapping behaviour, pupils need to appreciate the value of learning from mistakes and experience this in a classroom where mistakes are not associated with losing self-worth or feeling stupid and somehow diminished.

Case study 2.4: Valuing the pupil as a learner

Jonathan was reflecting on underachievement and self-handicapping behaviour and commented to fellow teachers in the staffroom:

> I appreciate that it is important to learn from mistakes and I try to create a classroom environment where all comments are valued. I realise it is not just what I say, but what I don't say and what my body language communicates to the pupil. It is from this that the pupils get a sense of whether their comments and themselves as a learner are valued. But it is much more difficult getting the pupils to respect and value each other's comments.

Discussion points

a. How do you show pupils that you value their comments? In answering this you may want to refer to the following types of verbal and non-verbal praise (Bani 2011).
   i. specific verbal praise
   ii. giving tangible rewards, e.g. stickers
   iii. complimenting pupils to the class or other member of staff
   iv. eye contact, facial expressions (such as smiling/laughing/winking), nodding, thumbs-up or other signs of approval
   v. one-to-one attention
b. From your observation, how do pupils value each other's comments? Again, you need to pay attention to both verbal and non-verbal responses.
c. What can you do to foster a culture of respect? (You may wish to consider communities of practice, pp. 15–16.)

Covington's (1992) self-worth theory reflects the theories of Marsh et al. (1978) and Hargreaves (1967, 1982) which talk of a need for pupils to make their mark and suggests that if they cannot succeed in a formal academic sense pupils will turn to other areas in which they can prove their worth. Marsh and Hargreaves argue that disaffection, a lack of motivation to engage in classroom activities, results in part from the school and teaching staff's inabilities to meet pupils' need for recognition. Staff involved in supporting teaching and learning will often give examples of pupils who are disengaged from the academic side of school but seem to have great skills in leadership and manage to have a following of other pupils. Marsh and colleagues argue that these disaffected, challenging pupils are, in the words of Galloway, et al., 'not lacking in motivation: they may if anything be too well motivated and thereby unwilling to accept failure in the school system in a resigned way' (Galloway et al. 1998, p. 98).

In order to engage a wider range of pupils, schools have looked to Gardner's theory of multiple intelligence (1993, 2006). According to this theory, pupils have the opportunity to be successful, and feel good about themselves, in a number of areas including logical/mathematical, interpersonal, intrapersonal, visual/spatial, body/physical, musical, naturalistic and verbal/linguistic.

It is important to remember that, as individuals, we each have a unique range of abilities and that we will use them with varying degrees of effort.

Gilbert (2002, pp. 178–179) argues that there are a number of benefits to be derived from the creative use of teaching following Gardner's theory of multiple intelligences (see Table 2.6), and that these include:

- Giving pupils a chance to show their teachers what they can do, which in turn impacts on teachers' expectations.
- Giving pupils a chance to show their classmates what they can do. This can assist with social inclusion within the classroom by demonstrating to all pupils that each person is unique with a talent or talents.
- Gives the pupil a chance to show themselves what they can do, leading to feelings of competency or self-efficacy and an 'I can do this attitude'.

Teaching in a manner that enables every pupil to have the opportunity to shine is part of good teaching practice, but perhaps what is more important and harder to develop within pupils is a strong internal belief in doing your best. Gilbert (2002, p. 28) discusses that 'Japanese culture has a form of internal motivation known as 'mastery', which involves trying to be no better than anyone other than yourself.' Gilbert links this view to the notion of being one's own personal best in the field of sports and Mihaly Csikszentmihalyi's (1990) concept of 'ipsative assessment' whereby the focus is on assessing individual performance against prior performance, i.e. 'am I better today than I was yesterday?' Without a doubt, this manner of thinking is extremely beneficial, and initiatives such as *Assessment for Learning* (Assessment Reform Group 2002), with the emphasis on pupil self-assessment, focus on this notion of continuous improvement. What those involved in teaching would like to read in terms of a pupil's self-assessment would be something like:

> I am proud of what I handed in. Regardless of the mark I receive I have learnt so much from the process of doing this assignment. I will take on what others say and seek to do even better next time.

Again, the challenge for those involved in teaching is how to enable a pupil to develop this attitude. A teacher and teaching assistant can role model this by living up to these goals/standards themselves and by sharing with pupils positive examples of the way in which they, themselves, think about learning challenges.

Table 2.6 Multiple intelligences

Type of multiple intelligence	Definition	Classroom activities that draw upon various types of intelligences
Spatial	This intelligence involves spatial judgement; that is, the ability to visualise with the mind's eye. Individuals with this intelligence could become artists, designers, and architects.	Visual displays, learning maps, colour coding work.
Linguistic	This intelligence focuses on the ability to communicate through words, spoken or written. Such individuals excel at reading, writing, telling stories and learning languages.	Listening, reading, discussing, debating, writing.
Logical mathematical	This intelligence focuses on the ability to apply logic and reasoning to abstract patterns and problems. Individuals with this type of intelligence will excel in activities involving maths.	Generating rules; completing puzzles; creating charts, graphs; conducting analysis.
Bodily-kinaesthetic	This intelligence focuses on an individual's ability to control bodily movements and to manipulate objects skilfully. Such individuals excel in athletics and dance.	Movement; acting; making things.
Musical	This intelligence focuses on auditory sensitivity, recognition and manipulation of sounds, rhythms and tones.	Listening, listening to forms of music, learning academic material through songs, chants, raps, etc.
Interpersonal	This intelligence focuses on the ability to relate to other people. These individuals are sensitive to others' moods and feelings and this sensitivity enables them to get on and work well with others.	Any type of group work, team work, collaborative learning, leading, role playing, instructing others.
Intrapersonal	This intelligence focuses on the ability to be self-aware and self-reflective.	Target setting, suitable to tasks which necessitate empathy.
Naturalistic	This intelligence focuses on the ability to relate to, and appreciate, natural surroundings or the environment.	Learning academic material by relating it to the environment and going out into the natural environment to learn.

Discussion points

Questions for teachers, teaching assistants, pupils and everyone:

a. Have I done my best?
b. Was there more that I could have done?
c. Am I proud of what I have achieved?
d. Am I better in some way than I was yesterday?
e. What can I do to improve?

As a note of caution, it is important to remain hopeful and positive when reflecting on whether one has done one's best. It would be tempting for both a pupil and teacher/teaching assistant to reflect on a particularly difficult day and to admit that they had not done their best, that there was more to done and that they feel inadequate. The key is to focus on the question 'Am I better in some way than I was yesterday?' and to realise that there has been progress.

The power of expectations

In this chapter we have talked at length about the attributions or explanations pupils make about their behaviour. However, we have not discussed the impact that teachers' and teaching assistants' beliefs and attitudes can have on pupils' attitudes.

It is helpful to consider how attitudes, and in particular how beliefs about how we define ourselves, are formed. Cooley (1902) in his 'looking glass theory' described how we look to others to define ourselves. In a sense, how we define ourselves is a reflection of 'how we think others see us'. Mead (1934), expanding on this theory, stated that, in time, how we believe specific people see us becomes internalised, forming a general view of how everyone sees us – and that our view of ourselves is constantly shifting and being updated by the everyday interactions we have with important others, such as friends, parents and teachers. Harter (1982) believes that we define ourselves in a number of ways: cognitive competence (how intelligent we are), social competence (how popular we are), physical competence (how good at sports or games we are) and general self-worth (how good a person do we feel we are).

At this point, we turn to the power of expectations.

A classic study in this area, which was conducted by Rosenthal and Jacobson (1966), examined the impact of labelling, teacher expectations and 'the self-fulfilling prophecy'. In this well documented study the researchers went into a school and administered an intelligence test to all pupils and, on the basis of this test, informed teachers that some pupils were 'academic bloomers' (that is, these pupils were expected to come on in leaps and bounds, academically speaking). Sure enough, when the researchers returned a year later these academic bloomers had improved dramatically. However, the catch was that the researchers had lied and the pupils whom they had defined as academic bloomers were in fact chosen randomly from the school register. What this study showed was the powerful effect of expectations; what is now known as 'the self-fulfilling prophecy'. It is important to consider why positive expectations had this dramatic effect.

According to the 'looking glass theory', if how we define ourselves is a reflection of how others see us, then perhaps the pupils picked up on their teachers' expectations that they would succeed and came to believe it themselves.

In terms of attribution theory, if pupils believed that teachers saw them as having the potential to achieve, then perhaps they tried harder and persevered with challenging learning tasks.

Perhaps the teachers believing the pupils would succeed spent more time with them, asking them more probing questions and helping them to develop their responses to questions – and therefore gave more time to developing their learning.

Perhaps the teachers praised the pupils more creating a warmer and more nurturing learning environment.

This study clearly demonstrated the power of positive expectations. However, there were some caveats in that the power of expectations seemed to have a greater impact on younger pupils.

If expectations can have positive effects, then the reverse is also clearly true. One teacher in describing her challenges in teaching a lower set maths class stated, 'I realised that not only had the pupils given up, but I as their teacher had given up on them.'

Here we see a complex interaction between the teacher/teaching assistant and the pupils.

If teachers/teaching assistants believe pupils have failed due to lack of ability, then their motivation to work with, ask probing questions of, help develop answers and encourage pupils' work is diminished.

Pupils' response to low expectations can be to become less motivated and engaged which the teacher can interpret as further evidence of low ability – which further justifies the low expectations.

For a teacher/teaching assistant, it is not only important to examine pupil motivation but to interrogate his or her own motivation to encourage pupils.

Case study 2.5: The nurturing classroom – can a positive relationship conquer all?

A nurturing classroom where the teacher/TA communicates to the pupil that he or she is are valued will, of course, have a positive impact on the pupil's sense of self-worth and willingness to engage with learning. Value can be communicated through both verbal and non-verbal means.

A recent TV documentary showed a secondary teacher ending his lesson by saying to his class 'clear off scumbags'. On watching the programme, it was clear that this comment was said within the context of a positive relationship.

Is it then that it is not *what* the teacher/teaching assistant says but *the manner in which it is said*?

Is the relationship between a teacher/teaching assistant and pupil so powerful that, if a relationship is strong, any strategy would be effective?

Likewise, can a good strategy be effective if there is not a positive relationship between the pupil and member of staff?

Setting goals

Much has been written about setting goals in order to enhance motivation and, indeed, much of the initiatives involving *Assessment for Learning* focus on pupils setting their own goals or targets. Locke and Latham (1990), in their goal-setting theory, see all human action as purposeful and, therefore, human action requires goals to be set and assumes that individuals will actively pursue these goals. However, goals differ in terms of how specific they are, the level of difficulty and the individual's commitment to the goal. Locke (1996) in describing the nature of goal setting stated:

- More difficult goals lead to perceptions of greater achievement.
- The more specific or detailed the goal, the easier it is to monitor performance and progress in meeting the goal.
- Goals that are both specific and difficult produce the greatest sense of achievement.
- Commitment to goals is more important and necessary when goals are specific and difficult. Less commitment is needed when goals are easy or vague. A vague goal does not require much commitment as vague goals can be achieved by both redefining the goal (moving the goalposts, so to speak) and by minimal performance.
- High commitment to goals is attained when an individual sees the goal as valuable and doable. (Cited by Dornyei 2001, p. 26.)

Most educational professionals are familiar with the terminology 'SMART' in reference to goals, i.e. that goals should be Specific, Measurable, Achievable, Realistic, and have a designated Timeframe. But, again, there has been debate regarding whether pupils' goals should be realistic or whether pupils should aspire for something more challenging; that is, aim for the stars.

Case study 2.6: Being realistic or aiming for the stars?

Sam was involved in working with a bottom set science class. The predicted GCSE grades for the pupils Sam was supporting were low. Most were predicted to get a handful of Ds and Es at best; however, when talking to the pupils, the pupils all had great plans.

Joe loved animals and was determined to become a vet.

Sadie loved watching crime programmes on TV and said she saw herself as a forensic psychologist.

As Jade was actively involved in caring for her mother, who had complex health needs, Jade wanted to become a doctor.

Although these pupils knew their predicted grades, this did not deter them from having these plans for what they wanted to do once they finished school. Sam really did not know what to say to them. Should she try to get them to be realistic and crush their dreams – or should she advise them to revise their career plans, knowing that they were unlikely to achieve the necessary GCSEs?

What should Sam say?

Gilbert (2002) states that the argument for *not encouraging pupils to aim high* is due to the perceived fear of professionals that pupils will not be able to handle the disappointment of not meeting their goals. Some argue that teachers, in trying to protect less able pupils' self-esteem, do not insist that pupils work to their full potential and thus expect too little. This may protect self-esteem, but it does not give pupils the academic skills that they need to succeed. Gilbert (2002, p. 25) advocates that pupils should not be told what they can or cannot do in a world in which anything is possible, and that they should be taught 'to aim high and develop strategies to cope with things not working out as planned'. Here, again, we return to the theme of the importance of learning how to deal with mistakes and failures in a positive manner.

Intrinsic versus extrinsic motivation

At this point, it is important to return to a discussion on intrinsic versus extrinsic motivation. To recap, intrinsic motivation involves engaging in an activity for its own sake and those pupils who are intrinsically motivated work on tasks because they find them enjoyable. On the other hand, those who are extrinsically motivated ask the question 'what's in it for me' and engage in an activity to gain rewards, stickers, merit points, teacher praise or to avoid sanctions such as detentions.

Much has been written on both forms of motivation, and there has been considerable debate as to which is more beneficial to the activity of learning and whether the development of one form of motivation detracts from the other.

Here we return to the important consideration of whether:

- Intrinsic motivation is the holy grail of motivation.
- Intrinsic motivation is better than extrinsic motivation – that is, do pupils learn more and better if they are learning because they personally enjoy the topic or could they learn equally well if they are engaging in the activity to gain a house point, earn money or just to stop their parents nagging?
- The consequence of creating a classroom environment in which rewards and sanctions play an important role is to possibly diminish the degree of intrinsic motivation that pupils have. So, if a pupil enjoyed working on maths worksheets and then was rewarded for completing the task, would they still enjoy working on maths worksheets?

Before considering these issues, it is necessary to differentiate the concepts of intrinsic and extrinsic motivation from the concept of interest (Schunk et al. 2010). Interest in the context of classroom behaviour can be defined as a preference for liking and wanting to engage in an activity (Schraw and Lehman 2001). Interest is not a type of motivation but a factor that influences motivation. Urdan and Turner (2005) discuss two types of interest, one being personal interest, which is a stable personal preference for an activity, and 'situational interest', which represents a more temporary state of attention to a topic. Obviously, good teaching involves devising effective lessons that create situational interest in a topic and thereby effectively engaging all pupils in lesson tasks. Teaching can influence motivation by making learning interesting.

But back to the discussion regarding intrinsic motivation, if this is a quality that those involved in teaching should be aiming to develop in their pupils to what extent can this be developed and more importantly how?

Pupils' motivation to learn can take many forms, but the research (Gottfried 1990; Lepper et al. 2005) does suggest that those pupils who are intrinsically motivated do learn and achieve more, have higher perceptions of personal competence and experience less anxiety in relation to learning. Therefore, intrinsic motivation should be encouraged and developed.

Lepper et al. (2005) state that it is tempting *but incorrect* to see intrinsic and extrinsic motivation as opposite points on a line or a continuum. For example, it would be incorrect to assume that if a person is engaged in an activity out of pure enjoyment (that is, highly intrinsically motivated), then they must have no regard or need for any form of reward. The relationship between intrinsic motivation and extrinsic motivation is more complex. The authors state that it is more helpful to see intrinsic and extrinsic motivation as separate factors, in that a pupil can experience both extrinsic and intrinsic motivation in reference to the same activity at the same time.

Consider a skilled artist or an accomplished musician or athlete. Why do they do what they do? Obviously most artists would be intrinsically motivated, but are money, fame and status of no importance? The important point here is that, for any activity, pupils can experience both intrinsic and extrinsic motivation.

Theory of self-determination

The theory of self-determination (Ryan and Deci 2000) acknowledges that not all behaviours can be intrinsically motivated and that behaviours in schools, as in society, are controlled by external rules and structures. In schools, external structures include school timetables and behaviour policies which describe systems of rewards and sanctions. Indeed, to fit into society, individuals need to conform to external rules and, to begin with, conformity can be regulated or controlled by rewards and non-conformance punished by sanctions. In schools, to begin with, doing work is rewarded by stickers and inappropriate behaviour such as rudeness is dealt with by sanctions such as having to stay in at break time. However, in time these forms of external regulations can become internalised and part of how a pupil regulates or controls his or her own behaviour. Ryan and Deci (2000) describe four types of extrinsic motivation:

- *External regulation*: At this level, the pupil is dependent on external sources of motivation, such as stickers, teachers or parental praise. Pupils at this stage might say: 'I do my work so I will get a sticker' or 'I do my work so I won't get a detention.'
- *Introjection*: Here the pupil has, to a certain extent, internalised rules. At this stage the pupil is still motivated by the approval of others and fears of disapproval; however, now there is what Ryan and Deci (2000) describe as ego involvement. Ego involvement simply means that the pupils now have an inner ability to praise and punish themselves. Pupils at this stage might say: 'If I don't hand in my assignment I will feel guilty' or 'When I hand in my assignment I will feel great.'
- *Identification*: At this stage, a pupil engages in an activity because he or she highly values and identifies with the behaviour and sees its usefulness. Pupils at this stage might say: 'I am spending hours and hours revising for my 'A' Level exams as I need to get three grade As to go to university.'
- *Integration*: At this level, the pupil engages in an activity because he or she sees the activity as important to his or her sense of self. For example, a pupil might say: 'I draw and paint because that is who I am.'

Integrated regulation is close to intrinsic motivation, but with intrinsic motivation there is no specific gain from engaging in the activity other than from an internal sense of pleasure.

This is an interesting theory, in that it suggests that over time extrinsic forms of motivation, such as verbal praise by a teacher, can become internalised. This theory has important implications, in that those involved in teaching should be striving to encourage pupils to internalise systems of rewards, so that ultimately the pupils reward themselves.

Case study 2.7: From external to internal regulation

I was working in year 1. I asked a child to tidy away her play equipment and she told me in no uncertain terms that she would only do this if she got a sticker. I was horrified by this use of bargaining at such a young age.

However, after reading Deci and Ryan's theory on types of extrinsic motivation, I realised that this behaviour reflected a type of motivation (external regulation). But, I also realised that I had a role to play in helping to develop pupils' internal regulation or how they controlled their own behaviour. I still give stickers, but now I also encourage young pupils to create their own stickers in order to praise themselves.

What would you do?

If intrinsic motivation is something to strive for, how do teachers and teaching assistants recognise intrinsic motivation in their pupils? Harter and Connell (1984) believed that you could measure the degree to which pupils were intrinsically motivated, as such pupils would:

- Prefer challenging rather than easy work. The challenging work chosen would be achievable.
- Explain that they work to satisfy their own curiosity and interest rather than obtaining teacher praise or good marks.
- Independently choose to engage in challenging activities and make mastery attempts; that is, have a go at challenging activities. These pupils would prefer not to be dependent on a teacher for deciding when and what to work on.
- Make independent judgments on the value of their work rather than depending on a teacher's judgment.
- Set internal standards for success or failure. (Adapted from Schunk et al. 2010, pp. 240–241.)

Harter's work on how intrinsic motivation develops has relevance for teaching and learning.

To backtrack, Harter saw intrinsic motivation as part of a more general process which is termed 'effectance motivation'. Effectance motivation assumes that individuals need to feel competent in their interactions with their environment and that this type of motivation leads to 'mastery attempts'; that is, behaviour designed to control their environment. Harter believed that this need to feel competent was reflected in various areas of life, including academic achievement, social relationships and athletic skills.

What is of interest regarding effectance motivation is how it develops as the child matures and how it is influenced by 'socialising agents' such as parents, teachers and teaching assistants. What is crucial to developing this inner sense of competence is what happens when the child makes a mastery attempt.

Examples of mastery attempts for a child just beginning school could include learning to tie his shoe laces, riding a bike or writing his name. Positive outcomes for mastery attempts would involve reinforcements such as praise and approval. To develop an inner sense of competence, socialising agents are needed to model mastery attempts i.e. to show the child how to act or what to do. Independence in attempting goals is rewarded by the socialising agents; being dependent is not. To begin with, parents should encourage mastery attempts that involve a challenging task that is not too hard or too easy. Over time, a child will internalise a self-reward system for his mastery attempts and this leads the child to feel that he is competent and in control. In turn, this strengthens his belief in his own competence or self-efficacy.

On the other hand, if a child's mastery attempts are met by failure, disapproval or criticism by others this can lead to a child feeling incompetent, helpless and that his life is controlled by outside forces. These children are anxious when faced with learning challenges. They lack an internal system of regulation or reward and therefore depend on others (teachers) to set goals and to reward their efforts.

Harter's theory sees it as the role of parents to encourage children to attempt suitably challenging activities. Eccles et al. (1998) state that parents can influence their child's motivation by being sensitive to his or her development, setting appropriate demands, showing the child that they have confidence in his or her ability, being emotionally supportive and by being highly motivated role models, willing to take on challenges themselves. Of course, teachers and teaching assistants can influence pupil motivation by following this advice.

Can pupils be punished by rewards?

One of the debates that revolve around concepts of intrinsic and extrinsic motivation is the role that rewards play. One line of argument hold that rewards diminish intrinsic motivation and there has been some research (Lepper and Greene 1978; Lepper and Henderlong 2000; Deci et al. 1999) that shows that pupils who are rewarded for engaging in an activity which they find enjoyable, over time lose their intrinsic motivation for engaging in the activity; that is, they enjoy the task less. This has important implications for the classroom, though, like much theory concerning motivation, the reasons behind such changes in heart and mind are complex.

One reason for this possible change in heart is the internal dialogue a pupil has regarding why he or she behaves in a certain way. Consider the following:

Young pupil: I love to draw and paint.
Teacher: Here is a sticker for a lovely painting.

Imagine that this situation is repeated every time that the young child creates a painting. The young child will think 'I love to paint and I like getting stickers.' Now imagine a situation where the child then does not get a sticker. The young child may think 'I didn't get a sticker. Why am I painting? I don't like painting anymore! Why am I painting?'

In the example above, the cognitive evaluation theory (Deci 1975; Deci and Moller 2005) states that rewards have the potential to both control and inform, and it is how the pupil interprets these aspects that is crucial. So, back to the example: the young child could view the reward as controlling his or her behaviour – 'The reason that I am painting is to get a sticker.'

This interpretation of the reward could diminish intrinsic motivation if the child believed the only reason he is painting is to receive stickers. In this case, if the child no longer received stickers for painting he may see no point in continuing to paint, as given in the example.

However, there is another possibility in that rewards are communicating information about how the activity is being carried out, i.e. information regarding the pupil's performance. Here, the young child could be saying to himself 'The reason for getting the sticker is that I am getting better at painting.'

This interpretation focuses on the fact that the reward is giving the child information about his performance, and this positive information can lead to the pupil feeling more competent about himself. Indeed, in some cases extrinsic reward or praise can be internalised and lead to greater intrinsic motivation.

At the beginning of this discussion, the importance of both the pupil's internal dialogue and how he interpreted the impact of the reward was stressed. What cognitive evaluation theory powerfully shows is the need for teachers and teaching assistants to highlight the reason for the reward. A reward is not given just for participating in the activity but should signify to the pupil that you, the teacher or teaching assistant, have recognised the pupil's effort and achievement.

Cognitive Evaluation theory can explain why sometimes pupils can be punished by rewards and why under certain circumstances rewards can enhance intrinsic motivation.

Discussion points

a. When do you give out rewards, and on what basis?
b. In reference to the pupils you work with – what are their perceptions of the rewards?

Developing intrinsic motivation by engaging curiosity

Possible ways in which intrinsic motivation can be developed include:

*   Challenge: presenting pupils with tasks that are not too difficult, nor too easy.
*   Curiosity: presenting pupils with surprising information that will inspire them to find out more.
*   Control: providing pupils with choices in regard to how they learn.
*   Fantasy: introducing an element of fun by encouraging imaginative thought through learning activities that involve games and simulations (Schunk et al. 2010, p. 265).

Case study 2.8: Starting with and building on points of curiosity

Sadie and others in her school were discussing aspects of the Early Years Curriculum for the upcoming year. Her school decided to pilot an initiative whereby, before a topic was introduced, letters home were sent out asking parents to discuss with their sons or daughters 'what they already know about the topic and what they would like to find out', and, importantly, to return these suggestions and feedback to the school. The topic for the half-term was 'water' and, while the teachers thought they knew what questions would be asked, there were definite surprises. For example, some pupils were interested in finding out why the sea was salty, why cut flowers die even if they are kept wet and where water went when it goes down the plughole. In evaluating the new initiative, the Early Years teachers felt that learning was enhanced by using points of curiosity as a place to begin learning.

(Smith 2010)

Dornyei (2001, p. 18) stated that motivation is at its highest state when pupils feel 'competent, have sufficient autonomy, set worthwhile goals, get feedback and are affirmed by others'.

One important aspect of this is the notion of sufficient autonomy or control and, indeed, much has been written about what pupil control and autonomy would look like in the classroom.

De Charms (1968, 1976), in discussing how the environment made individuals think about the control that they had, described a theory that saw people acting as *origins* or as *pawns* depending on how they perceived their environment.

Pawns believed that they were under the control of external forces or others who would push them around, decide what, how and when things would happen and how they should respond. An environment in which an individual would feel like she was a pawn would be a prison – but would pupils perceive school as a prison? Origins, on the other hand, felt that they were in control, that they had personal autonomy and a say in what happened to them.

Important to this theory is that acting as a pawn or origin is not a personality trait but shifts or changes with the environment in which a person is placed and, of course, this theory has implications for the classroom. De Charms (1976) described a programme whereby teachers were taught ways in which they could encourage 'origin' behaviours in pupils by teaching skills involving setting realistic goals, developing specific plans to achieve goals and how to evaluate goal progress. De Charms felt that, in order for teachers to encourage origin behaviour in their pupils, they must first believe that they themselves were in control and thus could act as origins.

An origin-facilitating classroom would involve:

- Pupils being presented with choices, but the teacher would decide upon the range and type of choices offered.
- Personal responsibility must be developed within pupils.
- Pupils, once making a choice in regard to an activity, would be required to complete the activity. In evaluating the activity, teachers would need to encourage personal responsibility in not letting pupils blame others for their failures or to explain successes as being the result of luck.

Gilbert (2002) discussed the need for control in the classroom. He argued that this did not imply teachers throwing away lesson plans or giving complete control to pupils, but, rather, planning lessons so that pupils perceived or felt that they did have some control or choice.

When teachers and pupils give up – motivation dialogue

Case study 2.9: 'I promise it won't happen again – I will change'

Sarah was responsible for pastoral support at her school, and often worked with the most troubled and disaffected of the pupils. In her school, these pupils were described as 'high profile'. At times she had to admit that she felt like giving up as, no matter what she did, it did not seem to make a difference. If only she had a penny for every time a pupil would assure her that he would change and that it would not happen again – but it always did. And for the parents – well, often they too had become disillusioned upon hearing yet another strategy or plan. Often parents would comment 'Why should this work when nothing has worked so far? We have heard all this before!' From the other teachers she would often hear comments such as 'the die is cast'. It seemed as if everyone, including herself, had given up hope that things would ever change. For Sarah, what marked a turning point was training on motivational interviewing.

Motivational interviewing is a counselling technique that aims to 'address a lack of motivation to change in a structured and positive manner' (McNamara 1999, p. 140). This technique was originally used with patients who had been referred to clinics for substance abuse problems and eating disorders. Motivational interviewing recognised that the process of change was both difficult and complex and that, to begin with, a client may not see the need for change – in fact, he or she may deny that they have a problem. When this technique is applied to educational environments, it is often the teachers and parents that may first recognise that there is a problem and a need for change, before the pupil realises. For example, a pupil may skip classes and not be doing any work; this behaviour would be seen by the teaching staff as a major problem that could blight the pupil's future opportunities but the pupil may see his or her behaviour as giving status and credibility with the peer group. But how does change occur?

Motivational interviewing techniques aim to facilitate change by promoting pupil knowledge and concern regarding the behaviour to the point at which the pupil sees for himself a need for change. Once the need for change is recognised, motivational interview techniques attempt to promote pupils' beliefs in their capacity to change by promoting feelings of self-efficacy and healthy attributions. To recap, healthy attributions involve having high effort attributions, i.e. pupils realising that their efforts can make a difference and through effort that they can change. Motivational interviewing techniques encourage pupils to work through a model of change developed by Prochaska and DiClemente (1982) (as seen in Table 2.7).

Case study 2.10: Changing attitudes

Reflecting on the difference that motivational interviewing has made to her school and practice, Sarah noted that before her frustration at a lack of pupil progress stemmed from the fact that she, personally, was at the active change part of the process, in that she had an action plan worked out and was ready for change. However, she realised that the change process was complex and that often the pupils she worked with were at the pre-contemplation stage in which they did not see that there was even a problem, and that getting them to the contemplation stage took time. Not only did the pupils need to change, but she, as a teacher, needed to change the way she saw the change process in order to be more hopeful for the pupils she worked with – and hopeful that what she was doing could make a difference.

Table 2.7 Model of change

Stage	Definition	Example
Precontemplation	Individual does not recognise that a problem exists.	Skipping classes is not seen as a problem.
Contemplation	The individuals is willing to consider that there is a problem; that his behaviour is causing him to suffer in some ways and a change could be beneficial.	Here the pupil is actively thinking about the consequences of his actions and considers the implications of not attending classes (perhaps he may not be able to continue on to the sixth form as he had hoped) and that maybe he does need to change his attitude.
Determinism	Here the individual makes a decision to carry on as before or that he is ready for, and committed to, change.	If the motivational interview techniques have been successful the pupil agrees to change.
Active change	Here the individual begins an action plan designated to lead to change.	The pupil formulates an action plan in terms of attending class and completing homework. The pupil begins to work towards this plan.
Maintenance	New positive behaviour continues to be supported.	The pupil continues to work on attending classes and his effort is praised by staff.
Relapse	After a period of success, there is often a relapse where the individual returns to previous patterns of behaviour. This is an expected part of the change process and needs to be seen as such. The individual, with support from others, needs to return to the action plan.	Everything falls apart. The pupil skips school for a week and feels like a total failure and wants to give up. He is reassured by others that this is a normal part of the change process and to return to his action plan.

Value theories

As discussed in the previous section on motivational interviewing and the model of change, in order to change a pupil first needs to see the value of changing. Expectancy-value theories of motivation state that the likelihood that a pupil will engage in a learning task will be determined by both whether they thought they could do the task and whether they wanted to do the task. The aspect of whether a pupil wants to do a task is determined by the value that he or she places on the task. Eccles and Wigfield (1995) felt that this value depended upon:

- *Attainment value:* how important is it to master a skill or accomplish a task?
- *Intrinsic value:* does engaging in the activity lead to a personal sense of pleasure?

- *Extrinsic utility value*: does the pupils see the value and relevance of the task? Does the pupil see the task connecting to current and future goals?
- *Cost:* what is the price of engaging in the activity in terms of time, effort and emotional costs such as anxiety and fear of failure – and how would participating in this goal impact on other goals?

An interesting point for consideration is the extent to which teacher enthusiasm can impact on the value pupils place on learning.

Case study 2.11: Can teacher enthusiasm make a difference?

Enthusiasm and engagement as a starting point

Josie reflected on the statement that 'enthusiasm is contagious'. She noted that when she was feeling down her pupils would say, 'What's up with you – you are really in the dumps today, Miss.' Not surprisingly, when Josie was like this she found that the pupils were not interested in the lesson. Josie did admit that there were times when she had to teach aspects of the curriculum which she personally felt were boring and 'cringe-worthy'. Sometimes she would even say to the pupils, 'I know this is boring, but we have to do it!' But perhaps, if enthusiasm was infectious, she needed to be more enthusiastic. If she couldn't find value or relevance in the topic, how could she expect her pupils to find it? Perhaps if she was enthusiastic and enjoyed the lesson, then perhaps so would the pupils.

'All singing and dancing'

Josh was reflecting on the outcome of an observation he had as part of his performance management. Josh reflected that he had put his heart and soul into a particular lesson and still the lesson had been graded as being only satisfactory. The member of the senior management had acknowledged that he was charismatic and enthusiastic but said that he needed to focus more on pupil engagement. Josh, on some level, could see his point but then he had read that enthusiasm was contagious and he wanted the pupils to be as enthusiastic about the subject as he was. The member of the senior management team who had conducted the observation said that, though the pupils were quiet and seemed interested, they were not sufficiently engaged in the lesson. Josh, on reflection, acknowledged that the lesson was 'all singing and dancing', but that he was doing most of the singing and dancing himself.

Case study 2.12: The role of interest

Dianna asked her adult education class to reflect on which classes or learning situations led to their greatest amount of learning.

Daniel: School was boring. I struggled to learn anything in that environment. The teachers just read from text books.

Dianna: Should teachers try to make lessons interesting?

Daniel: Well it would help.

Alf: I remember some of the most inspiring lessons I had were in Biology – it wasn't the teacher, in fact he was very old fashioned and boring, but it was the subject matter that really sparked my curiosity. It was my curiosity that got me going.

Jane: Well I learnt best in this French class. The teacher was really strict and really boring but I can honestly say I learnt the most in her class. When I realised I was learning then I became interested, but would I have been interested if she hadn't been so strict in the first place?

Dianna: Yes, you may be learning in a lesson where the teacher is strict and boring, but are you really learning? Are you just producing work? Are you learning out of fear? Are you learning to love learning? Are you learning to be an independent learner?

Jane: Yes, I can see your point. But I think in that class I learnt that learning is about putting your head down and getting on with the task and sometimes that is what you need to do in order to learn.

Discussion points

a. From your experience, what learning situations have led to the greatest amount of learning? (Hint: consider personal and situational interest, p. 47.)
b. From your experience, did teacher enthusiasm impact on the value you placed on learning?
c. In your experience, does good teaching now involve the teacher entertaining pupils?

Goal orientation theory

As discussed in the previous section, there are a number of factors (i.e. pleasure gained from the task and the cost of engaging in the task) that shape the value pupils place on a learning task. Related to the value of the goal are the *reasons* pupils give for wanting to achieve goals. This is referred to as goal orientation theory. Goal orientation theory aims to explain how pupils learn and perform in school, and has generated much research. Ames (1992), in summarising this research, states that there are two distinct approaches, one being a mastery orientation in which the pupil focuses on the process of learning and the other a performance orientation in which the pupil focuses on demonstrating ability, getting good grades and out-performing other pupils. When presented with learning challenges, a pupil will say different things to him or herself depending on his or her goal orientation.

Table 2.8 Optimal (positive) and less optimal (positive) statements

Mastery orientation	Performance orientation
Pupil focuses on the process of learning.	Pupil focuses on demonstrating ability, getting good grades and out-performing other pupils.
Examples of what pupils say: optimal statements	**Examples of what pupils say: less optimal statements**
I like tasks that I can learn something from, even if they are so hard that I get many wrong and make mistakes.	I prefer problems that aren't too difficult so that I don't get too many questions wrong. I like questions that are difficult enough to show that I am clever.
I work hard to learn.	I work hard to get a good mark.
Making mistakes is part of the learning process.	I really don't like making mistakes.
I work because I want to learn new things.	I like to show my teachers that I am smarter than other pupils. The best situation is when I am the only person who can answer the teacher's questions. The worse thing that could happen is to look stupid. My main aim is to avoid looking like I can't do the work.
Being successful means I learn interesting things.	I feel successful when I achieve the highest mark in the class.
I feel successful when learning makes me think and makes me want to find out more.	I feel successful when I am the smartest and know more than others.

(Adapted from Schunk et al. 2010, p. 185 which in turn is based on the work of Dweck (2000), Ames (1992), Midgley et al. (1998) and Nicholls (1990).)

Case study 2.13: Encouraging positive statements

After reading the information set out in the above table, the small team of teachers and teaching assistants at Every Village Primary School was discussing what they could do.

Jo: As I see it, we need to encourage positive or optimal statements.
Sadie: But don't you think it is just natural to want to choose a task where you have a chance of succeeding and that you don't want to make mistakes – and didn't someone say that those who strive for success choose tasks that are not too difficult nor too easy but challenging, and that we need to encourage students to choose those suitably challenging tasks?
Jo: I agree, but I think the point is that worrying about making a mistake can really hold you back; that is, the risk of feeling thick or stupid prevents you from trying or asking questions.

Karen: I hate making mistakes. I know I tell the pupils that mistakes are a part of learning but it is different when it's you.

Mike: I remember at school, when we had our work returned to us, that Sir would make a big fuss about handing the work out and calling out the mark and making comments as he did so. It was great for those who achieved good marks but, for those who didn't, it was horrible.

Jo: I think we need to model and discuss these self-statements with our pupils. Remember the concept of 'ipsative assessment' where you need to compare your performance against prior performance; that is, you need to say 'Am I better today than I was yesterday?' and 'Am I doing the best that I can?'.

Sadie: Ok – but how do we get pupils to say these positive statements and believe in them?

Jo: Sadie, we will work together. When I give out the next project to year 5 we are going to do a role play about what we hope to get out of the task. I will say I want to learn and you can talk about how you want to get good grades and not be seen as dumb.

Sadie: Ok, we will model how to say positive self-statements.

The beliefs that pupils hold about learning reflect what pupils believe about the nature of intelligence. Beliefs about intelligence influence how pupils respond when they are presented with challenging situations. Therefore, knowing how a pupil thinks about goals and how intelligence is formed can predict how a pupil will respond to learning challenges.

Dweck (2000, 2008b) outlined a complex model of goal orientation that saw in the amount of effort that a pupil was willing to invest in a challenging learning situation the result of a pupil's belief about the nature of intelligence, her goal orientation and her confidence in her own ability or intelligence. This model in outlined in Table 2.9.

Dweck believes that a pupil's mindset has profound impact on subsequent learning and performance in school and that a growth mindset should be encouraged in pupils to support their learning. Though some pupils who have a fixed mindset, are performance-driven and have high confidence in their abilities can achieve, there are certain learning situations in which this fixed mindset creates problems. Table 2.10 describes the characteristics of individuals with fixed or growth mindsets.

Table 2.9 Dweck's model of goal orientation

View of intelligence	Mindset	Type of goal	Confidence in intelligence	Behaviour in task situations
Entity: intelligence is fixed	Fixed	Performance. The focus is on demonstrating ability, getting good grades and out-performing other pupils.	If high: If low:	Seeks challenge. High degrees of persistence. Avoids challenge, gives up quickly.
Incremental: intelligence can change and develop	Growth	Learning goal. The focus is on the process of gaining knowledge.	If high or low:	Seek challenge and persists when learning is difficult.

(Dweck and Leggett 1988, Dweck 2000, Dweck 2008b (adapted from Schunk et al. 2010, p. 187.)

Table 2.10 Characteristics of fixed and growth mindsets

	Fixed mindset	Growth mindset
How important is it to look smart?	Pupils worry about how smart they are and what others will think of them. This performance anxiety can lead to pupils avoiding learning opportunities that appear too challenging in case they fail.	Pupils are more interested in learning rather than looking smart. These pupils are open to learning challenges regardless of how confident they are in their initial ability.
What is the relationship between effort and ability?	Pupils believe that if you have ability then you don't need to work as knowledge would just come with little effort. If you did have to work then this would mean that you didn't have the ability in the first place. Such views can lead to pupils who have high ability not working as hard as they need to in order to achieve. This can lead to high ability pupils underachieving as they have not put in sufficient work.	Pupils believe that working harder makes you smarter and therefore, effort increases ability.
How are setbacks and mistakes perceived?	If a pupil makes a mistake or has a setback he is likely to question whether he is, in fact, clever. These pupils see mistakes as a reflection of lack of ability.	If a pupil makes a mistake or has a setback then this is a signal for the pupil to try harder or to use another strategy.
When do you feel clever?	These pupils will state that they feel clever when they find something easy, they finish a task quickly without a mistake or when other pupils can't do what they can.	These pupils say that they feel clever when they have had to really struggle to learn, when they realise that through their effort they have made progress and when they have helped others to learn.
How motivated are these pupils?	Motivation to take on learning challenges is limited as these pupils believe ability is fixed and effort has no role to play.	Motivation to take on and persist with learning challenges is high due to pupils' belief that achievement is related to effort and strategies used.

(Dweck 2000, 2008b.)

Dweck (2000, 2008b) attributes the development of a fixed mindset to well-intentioned praise that fails to make the connection between ability and effort. Praising children and pupils is important, but praise needs to be considered as pupils need to develop a positive approach to learning that recognises the connection between ability and effort and that sees mistakes and setbacks as an important part of the learning process. This advice stems from research into attribution and attribution retraining (please refer back to pp. 36–38). A focus on a growth mindset stresses the importance of seeing mistakes as a starting point for learning and that taking personal responsibility for learning is crucial.

Case study 2.14: Reflecting on fixed and growth mindsets

After reading information about Dweck's views on fixed and growth mindsets, the small team of teachers and teaching assistants at Every Village Primary School were discussing what they could do.

Mike: This theory relates to what we were talking about in terms of optimal or positive self-statements.

Jo: I think fixed and growth mindsets are an interesting concept but what is most important is what we say to students in terms of our feedback.

Sadie: Ideally, we need to praise their effort when pupils really do try. But sometimes pupils really do try and still fail and then to say, well try harder, it's not enough. They might think 'Well, I tried and that didn't work, so I'll just give up.'

Jo: I agree as we work together I need to know your opinions on how much effort a pupil has put in.

Mike: We could say that what trying and not succeeding means is that you need to do something different.

Sadie: But you would need to help them, you just couldn't leave it to the pupil to figure it out themselves – or could you?

Jo: I agree that pupils will need support and some pupils more support than others. You could ask them what they think they could do differently or you could suggest something for them to do. What you want them to realise is that effort does make a difference.

Mike: You could remind them of the progress they have made when they have tried harder before.

To maximise potential, those supporting teaching and learning need to encourage a growth mindset in the pupils with which they work – but how does one do this? Dweck (2008a) has developed a programme entitled 'Brainology' in which she tries to teach pupils that the brain is a muscle and that, as a muscle, it can grow with practice.

Setting goals and keeping goals

In this chapter we have talked about the importance of setting goals. But, intuitively, we know that setting goals are only the first step, and that the hard bit is keeping to them. On a personal level we only need to remind ourselves of the countless unfulfilled New Year's resolutions we have made: the promises that, yes, we will go on that diet or that, yes, we will

Case study 2.15: Creating programmes on mindsets

Amanda was very impressed by the work of Carol Dweck and decided to try out some of her ideas on the secondary pupils with whom she worked. Amanda devised a training programme consisting of a series of PowerPoint slides, and each day she spent time with her home tutor group discussing how the brain, as a muscle, can be developed and how the students can improve their learning. On reflecting on the impact of the short programme, Amanda felt that for some pupils it did make a difference. Some pupils seemed to experience that light bulb moment when they realised 'yes, maybe I can learn', but for others the impact did not seem to make a difference. These pupils were not bothered and perhaps what these kids heard at school, that they could succeed if they tried, was undermined by what they heard at home. Indeed, some pupils would say as much: 'My mum says I'll never be able to do maths' and 'My Dad says I'm thick.' Many of these pupils saw no point in trying or in learning at school. Perhaps what would really benefit the school was delivering classes on fixed and growth mindsets to parents as well as to other pupils and staff.

This was Amanda's next project.

get up early and go jogging three times a week. Goals are easy to set but keeping to them is difficult. In discussing the ebb and flow of how motivated pupils feel at any one time, with regard to working at and keeping to their goals, there is a need for regulation or, better still, self-regulation on the part of the pupil. If a goal or task is *regulated* then its progress is monitored and controlled by external forces such as a teacher or teaching assistant telling a pupil why, how, when, where, what and with whom the task should be completed. *Self-regulation* refers to the process whereby pupils activate and sustain thought, behaviours and feelings that are geared towards keeping to and meeting goals. Zimmerman (2000) argues that self-regulation involves choices on the behalf of the pupil in how they attain the goal, and that it is more helpful to think in terms of degree of self-regulation rather than whether a particular pupil can self-regulate or not.

Regulation is not the same as motivation, but regulation of some form is needed for goals to be achieved. If a level of control, autonomy and choice lead to higher levels of motivation then pupils in the classroom should be encouraged to regulate their behaviour. However, skills involved in successfully self-regulating (specifically in self-observation, self-judgments and self-reactions) are skills that need to be developed over time; the work on Assessment for Learning certainly involves these processes (see Chapter 5). In terms of what happens in the classroom, to begin with tasks which pupils are given are regulated by the teacher or teaching assistant but, over time, for a pupil to become an independent learner, i.e. develop a sense of personal responsibility for his learning, he needs to become self-regulated in terms of how he sets, monitors and achieves his own goals. Pupils will differ in the degree of support that they need from the teacher/teaching assistant and it is important to give pupils choices in aspects of self-regulation (such as how the task is to be achieved) that are perceived as challenging, but not too challenging. If an individual pupil perceives that he is being given too many choices about what to do, he may become overwhelmed, not know what to do and give up.

Table 2.11 Degrees of regulation and self-regulation

Aspect of learning	Regulation	Self-regulation
Why engage in the task?	Task or goal set by teacher or teaching assistant.	Pupil realises that engaging in the task will fulfil self-goals and lead to feelings of self-competency.
How is the task to be achieved?	Strategy to be used and format of finished product specified/set by teacher or teaching assistant.	Pupil makes choices as to what strategy to use and what form the finished product will take. For example, the pupil decides whether the finished product will be a written assignment or a presentation.
When is the task to be finished? When is the goal to be achieved?	This aspect refers to time management. If this aspect is regulated by the teacher, the teacher will set the time limit – for example that the assignment is due in next Monday.	Pupils would have some choice regarding when to hand in the assignment.
What does the task involve?	This aspect involves breaking the task down into sub-tasks and monitoring progress made. The teacher can take control of this aspect by saying on Monday 'I want to see a draft outline', on Tuesday 'I want to see your introduction', and so on. The teacher or teaching assistant would evaluate and give feedback on the quality of the work and what needs to be done next.	The monitoring of progress is the responsibility of the pupil. This involves self-observation, i.e. the pupil observes her work in terms of frequency (how often am I working), intensity (how hard am I working) and quality (what am I producing). Self-judgment involves the pupil comparing what she is doing to meet her goal and asking herself if she is doing enough. Self-reactions involve pupil responses to their self-judgments. For example, if a pupil thinks they are not doing enough they may start to work harder.
Where should the work on the task be carried out?	This aspect involves how the learning environment is structured. For example, a teacher could say that he wants the work to be carried out in class time.	Here the pupil decides where she works on the task and how she structures her environment. For example, the pupil may say that 'As I work best in the library, that is where I will work on this assignment.'
With whom should the task be carried out?	Here the teacher/teaching assistant decides whether the pupil should be working by herself or in a group.	Here the choice of whether to work individually or in groups is left to the pupil.

(Adapted from Schunk et al. 2010, p. 154.)

Volition and resilience

Volition, though related to self-regulation, is described as a complex process 'that protects concentration and directs effort in the face of personal and/or environmental distractions' (Corno 1993, p. 16).

Case study 2.16: 'If I could just bottle it'

Mrs Salford, reflecting on her year 2 class, stated: 'I am just amazed at Rory's level of concentration. All the others at his table were playing up and arguing and Tom was even under the table grabbing at his legs, but Rory just sat there, head down and worked on his maths worksheet. What I want to know is what enables him to focus like that? If only I could bottle it and give it to other pupils.'

Theorists such as Heckhausen (1991) and Kuhl (1984) make a distinction between predecisional processing (the thinking that goes on before setting a goal) and postdecisional processing (activities we engage in after setting a goal). Postdecisional processing (Corno 1993) is part of motivational control or volition. Postdecisional processing involves strategies which maintain levels of motivation and deal positively with negative emotions that can diminish motivation or lead a pupil to just pack it all in and give up.

Table 2.12 Strategies to self-manage motivation and emotions

Motivation control	Emotional control
Break goals into sub-goals and reward self for achieving these sub-goals. For example, a long term goal might be to paint a picture for an art exhibition, but short term goals might be to spend two hours per day working on the painting. These rewards can be in the form of self-praise or something more substantial, like chocolate biscuits.	When experiencing negative emotions such as anxiety or frustration, maintain a sense of calm by techniques such as controlling breathing, thinking about breathing in and breathing out, counting to 10, or thinking of positive things.
Impress upon yourself the importance of the goal.	When things get tough recall similar past situations that were difficult, but where you did eventually succeed by sticking with it.
Visualise yourself completing the goal, for example, finishing the painting.	When visualising yourself completing the goals think about how good you will feel when you finally finish.
Monitor your work through self-observation, self-judgment and self-reactions.	Remind yourself of your abilities and strengths.
Analyse setbacks to decide on alternative strategies and plans.	Think about how you can make your work more exciting and fun.

(Material drawn from Corno 1993, adapted from Schunk et al. 2010, p. 159.)

To recap, volition describes the process of maintaining and directing concentration in the face of personal and/or environmental distractions. Resilience, however, refers to the skills and personal attributes that enable individuals to survive, function and achieve despite experiencing disadvantage and risk (Masten 2001). Depending on background factors some pupils will need to develop resiliency strategies if they are to succeed and flourish. A young resilient person should be able to believe and say:

'I am likeable and respect myself and others.' This phrase demonstrates cognitive resilience.

'I can find ways to solve problems and can control myself.' This phrase demonstrates behavioural resilience.

'I have people to love me and help me.' This phrase demonstrates emotional resilience.
(Grotberg 1995, p. 130)

Ways to develop resiliency skills will be discussed further in Chapter 6 (pp. 137–139).

The social aspect of motivation

In discussing motivation, there is a need to recognise that we are social animals and many of our motives stem from our relationships with others. Individual motivation focuses on fulfilling personal desires, gaining knowledge to satisfy curiosity and self-confidence in believing that one can learn. Social motivation, on the other hand, includes social welfare goals (being a productive member of society), social solidarity goals (behaving in such a way as to bring honour to your family) and social approval goals (doing well in order to gain approval from important others, such as peers or teachers) (Urdan and Maehr 1995). In discussing social motivation, we recall that Marsh et al. (1978) and Hargreaves (1967, 1982) talked of a need for pupils to make their mark and to be recognised by others. However, cultures can differ in the value they place on formal education, the importance of learning and the social support for academic learning that is offered by family and peers (Chen and Stevenson 1995). Again, social motivation relates to communities of practice (see Chapter 1, pp. 15–16).

An interesting dilemma for schools concerns how pupils value effort and achievement. Are high academic achievers seen as popular members of the school body or are they seen as swots or geeks? Do very bright pupils downplay their abilities and not try hard, so as to avoid unpopular labels – and what can teachers/teaching assistants do?

Case study 2.17: As if . . .

Jeff, a pupil, was presented with an award by the head teacher at the school assembly. The head, in addressing all members of the school, described how Jeff had had an outstanding year. Not only had he played well on the school hockey team but had achieved excellent results in all his subjects. Jeff, in accepting his award, thanked his teachers and, mindful of his position as a role model of others in the school, told the school audience that any of them could be where he was if only they believed in themselves, aimed high and worked hard. When Jeff returned to his tutor group he was received with a round of genuine applause and praise from his classmates.

Discussion points

a.   Does this happen in your school? Why – or why not?
b.   How are pupils who strive for success seen at your school?

Case study 2.18: Motivating the high achievers

Anwar thought that there would not be an issue motivating the high achievers; such pupils were a joy to teach as they had a deep personal interest or passion for the subject. Anwar taught science throughout the school; however, he had begun to realise that one of his star pupils did not seem to be happy. She always completed her work a lot quicker than the others and often seemed bored. Anwar felt he needed to sort this out.

In their talk, the student said, yes, she was indeed bored, and that when she finished her work early the other pupils would glare at her – and that they treated her differently. Anwar realised that, from the student's perspective, there was a conflict between her desire to do well and learn and her need to be accepted by the group. Anwar realised that he had not helped matters. In fact he did depend on her to answer questions and he had noted that other students would remark 'Why ask me – ask her – she always knows the answers.' To resolve this, Anwar created an after school club for science where he involved all interested students in challenging projects that they could work on in class once they had finished their set work. From the student's perspective, she was no longer bored and always had work to do in class. Consequently, she did not feel different from the other pupils.

Discussion points

In your experience have there been issues in motivating the high achievers? If so, how have you dealt with such issues?

Teachers and teaching assistants have a role to play in establishing group norms for the classroom environment. Norms specify what acceptable behaviour within a classroom involves. Educational research has shown (Dornyei 2001) that effective classroom management practices enhance pupils' sense of wellbeing and achievement and, therefore, promotes pupil motivation. Likewise, pupils often cite other pupils 'acting up' and 'behaving inappropriately' as reasons for them not being able to engage in the lesson (for further discussion, see pp. 90, 94). What can the school do to encourage a culture of achievement? Maehr and Midgley (1991) state that schools can create a climate where there is:

*   A whole school emphasis on accomplishment.
*   High expectations regarding pupil potential.
*   School-level authority and management structures.
*   A high sense of teacher competence or self-efficacy.

Complexity

What has been described in this chapter is a vast range of theories that explain aspects of motivation. However, in determining what motivates a particular pupil, and what you as a teacher/teaching assistant can do to influence the motivation of a class or a pupil, many factors need to be considered. From a pupil's perspective, there may be social/home or environmental factors as well as role models, parental and society attitudes to learning that impact on motivation. There are, within a pupil, factors such as specific learning difficulties, personality, personal interests, mindsets and thinking/attributional styles that would influence motivation. And, of course, there will be environmental factors such as school ethos, classroom dynamics, peer pressure and teacher/teaching assistant expectations.

Though these factors can be considered in isolation, the reality is that the factors that underlie motivation interact with each other and, therefore, to move forward in motivating yourself, other colleagues, pupils, the class or the school as many as possible factors, theories, explanations and strategies need to be considered. This is the challenge of motivation!!

Summary

- Pupils may be driven by a need to succeed or a need to avoid failure.
- Pupils give many explanations to explain personal successes and failures. These explanations include ability, effort, task difficulty, luck, mood, family background, help and distractions. However, the most common explanations focus on ability and effort.
- A healthy attribution style sees the pupil explaining successes in terms of personal effort and failure in terms of inappropriate effort and incorrect strategy use.
- Sometimes, in order to protect self-esteem a pupil may engage in self-handicapping behaviour, such as not studying for an exam, so that if he fails he can attribute failure to lack of effort.
- Pupils need to learn that a key feature of learning involves learning how to deal with failure, i.e. that making mistakes is part of the learning process.
- Pupils should be encouraged to aim high but be given strategies to cope effectively with setbacks. Teachers and teaching assistants can role model positive approaches to learning.

Chapter 3

Managing to collaborate

An overview

This chapter focuses on teachers and teaching assistants working collaboratively within the classroom (in addition to SENCos working collaboratively with multiple teacher/TA partnerships) in order to ensure high quality provision for pupils. But what is collaboration, why is collaboration needed and how are collaborative relationships established and maintained? Further, how can a collaborative relationship enhance motivation in the classroom?

The modern classroom is a very different place even compared to classrooms two decades ago, and part of the difference is the role that teaching assistants play. While, historically, the role of a teaching assistant involved sharpening pencils, cleaning paint pots and listening to pupils read, the role now sees teaching assistants requiring an understanding of how children develop and learn in order to effectively support teaching and learning in the classroom.

Teaching assistants are a valuable resource. In a comprehensive review of the impact of adult support staff on pupils and mainstream schools Alborz et al. (2009, p. 4) quoted Her Majesty's Inspectorate's 2002 'confirmation of the tremendous contribution that well trained and well managed teaching assistants can make to driving standards up in schools' and that the quality of teaching in lessons is higher when teaching assistants are present.

In order for teaching assistants to be used to their full potential, attention needs to be given to the nature of their deployment, i.e. how schools, SENCos and teachers work with teaching assistants on a day to day basis. However, though many teachers would now see their role as managing teaching assistants, there is a lack of specific training for teachers regarding the underpinning skills needed to work effectively with teaching assistants (Edmond 2003; Hammersley-Fletcher and Lowe 2005; Bubb and Earley 2006). It is the aim of this chapter to explore ways in which teachers and TAs can reflect on their working relationships.

Relationship to motivation

As stated in Chapter 2, motivation within a classroom context refers to a pupil's drive or energy to engage in an activity, and that motivation encompasses the choice of, persistence with, and effort expended on, an activity. Motivation not only refers to the decision to engage in an activity but the motivation to stay on task and to see the work through, especially if the going gets tough. Dornyei (2001, p. 35) sees the role of teachers as designated leaders within the classroom and that, as such, they 'embody group conscience, symbolise the group's unity and identity and serve as a model'. In short, the role of a teacher is to direct and energise; that is, to motivate the group.

As teachers need to direct and energise the pupils with whom they work, so teachers must direct and energise their own behaviour and, importantly, they must direct and energise the teaching assistants they work with.

Likewise, a teaching assistant, in supporting learning, acts to energise and direct pupils, realising that they need to also look at how they motivate themselves and that of other adults with whom they work.

And, of course, there is the role of the SENCo. A SENCo's responsibilities with regard to teaching assistants include recruitment and appointment, deployment, clarification of roles and responsibilities, building collaborative teams, induction, training, monitoring of work and performance management. Therefore a SENCo has a pivotal role in directing and energising the work of both teachers and teaching assistants.

To recap, whose motivation are we talking about? We are talking about the motivation of pupils, the motivation of staff and the complex interplay between each.

In looking at the dynamics of teacher and teacher assistant roles, we return to the imaginary story that began Chapter 2 (pp. 28–29). In this imaginary example, the lesson had not gone well and, though the teacher and teaching assistant had given brief feedback to each other (in that they agreed that the lesson was OK), there were silent recriminations.

Case study 3.1: What I say is not what I think

Ms Smythe (teacher) and Josie (teaching assistant) both agreed that, all considered, it had gone fairly well. But, privately, Josie thought that Ms Smythe needs to be stricter, she needs to show them who is the boss and the revision exercise was boring.

Privately, Ms Smythe thought that Josie just doesn't understand the complex nature of the pupils and how pupils learn and develop.

Though these recriminations were kept private, each suspected the other of holding these views.

Discussion points

There are several questions that emerge from this case study:

a. Does having these private views and not discussing them have any impact on pupil learning outcomes?
b. Does having these private views and not discussing them impact on the working relationship between the teacher and teaching assistant?
c. Does having these private views and not discussing them impact on their respective individual levels of motivation?

What is collaboration?

Before examining various definitions of collaboration it is helpful to look at the nature of the teacher/teaching assistant relationship. Numerous government documents (DfES 2000,

2001, 2003, 2004a, b and c) state that the role of the TA is to work under the guidance of a teacher. Specifically, Rose (2000) saw the role of the teaching assistant as overseeing the work of small groups of pupils, including those pupils with special educational needs, and the implementation of relevant interventions.

Of course, teachers and teaching assistants need to collaborate. Collaboration is a term that is often used, but what do we mean by it, and how does it develop? Indeed Devecchi (2005) advised that it may be more helpful to think about how adults go about supporting each other and the pupils.

However, there have been a number of definitions in relation to collaboration, including:

- To work jointly and to co-operate (Sykes 1986).
- From a teaching assistant's perspective, 'it's about working together for the good of the child and knowing my strengths, their strengths, and symbiotically existing in that room for the good of all of those children' (Bentham 2011).
- A process by which people work co-operatively together to accomplish a task, or a series of tasks, of benefit to one or more people by reaching a mutual understanding of how to solve problems and resolve complex ethical and practical dilemmas (Devecchi and Rouse 2010, p. 9).

Devecchi and Rouse (2010) further differentiate between a functional and a personal dimension of collaboration, though they see both dimensions being intertwined and impacting on each other.

Functional collaboration relates to technical knowledge on how to support teaching and learning that is shared by both the teacher and teaching assistant, while a personal dimension involves an affective knowledge of what is involved in collaboration, including the need for respect, reciprocal care and trust.

Returning to our imaginary example, important discussions regarding technical knowledge of how to support learners, i.e. what would be an appropriate and engaging lesson, are not being discussed due to a possible lack of trust.

A model of collaboration

Bentham (2011), through in-depth qualitative interviews with teachers and teaching assistants, developed a model of collaborative relationships. In this study, teachers and teaching assistants were asked a series of questions to determine how they defined a great, average and poor working relationship in terms of personal attributes, involvement in planning, feedback and understanding of learning. More importantly, they were asked how a collaborative relationship can move forward or improve.

In attempting to create a model of collaborative practice it is important to consider whether:

- All teacher and teaching assistants have collaborative working relationships and, if so, how these relationships differ in terms of quality.
- Collaborative working relationships only work if they are an outstanding relationship.
- There are individual differences in term of what teachers and teaching assistants describe as an ideal, average and poor relationship.
- A collaborative working relationship needs to be actively encouraged or will it develop naturally with time?

- The type of relationship one teacher or teaching assistant has can change or fluctuate over the course of time or even over one day (not to mention a term or a year).

Despite questions regarding the nature of collaborative relationships, in research conducted by Bentham (2011) there was agreement between those interviewed in terms of what was considered a great, average and poor relationship. However, you may read what follows and justifiably say 'I have a totally different opinion'. The important point to note is that what is proposed is a model (see Table 3.1) and, as such, a model attempts to provide teachers and teaching assistants with a starting point to look at, reflect and examine their own relationships.

Discussion points

How do you view a great, an average and a poor working relationship between teachers and TAs?

Look at the following line:

```
..........................................................................................................................
1                              5                                        10
```

Let's imagine that 10 is a great relationship, 5 is an average relationship and 1 is a poor or awful working relationship.

a. What is 10, a great relationship, in terms of TA involvement in planning, feedback between teachers and teaching assistants, personal qualities and TA understanding/skills?

b. What is 5, an average relationship, in terms of TA involvement in planning, feedback between teachers and teaching assistants, personal qualities and TA understanding/skills?

c. What is 1, a poor relationship, in terms of TA involvement in planning, feedback between teachers and teaching assistants, personal qualities and TA understanding/skills?

d. If an observer was in your classroom would they be able to just sit there and within 5 minutes say, 'Oh yes, this is a really good /average/poor working relationship'? What would they see?

e. What does a good working relationship feel like?

f. If a working relationship is at the lower end of the scale, how can the relationship improve? What can the teacher/TA/school do to improve the relationship?

(Bentham 2011)

Table 3.1 A proposed model of how teachers and TAs defined and classified collaborative relationships

Type of relationship	Great/outstanding	Average relationship	Awful/poor
Personal attributes	High levels of trust evident which impacts on quality of communication and improves quality of provision for pupils. Trust enables teachers/TAs to have more detailed discussions regarding how pupils learn and how they can learn from each other.	Trust developing – this trust enables teachers/TAs to have basic conversations about pupil learning characterised by 'this child couldn't understand this', but important details are missing.	Absence of trust. Without trust relationships are perceived as stressful.
Planning	The ideal would be to plan with the year group staff to include teachers and teaching assistants. TAs would be involved in planning and could help teachers to plan, receive, suggest and share ideas.	TAs have some input but do not attend teachers planning meetings. TA input characterised by 'adding in how we're going to deliver something, rather than coming up with ideas'.	No TA input or involvement in planning. TAs not listened to and ideas dismissed.
Feedback	TA feedback to teachers would focus on aspects of pupil learning, strategies used, pupil achievements, discussions regarding where to go next and resources needed. Teachers would give direct constructive feedback to TAs and 'both would be able to take criticism from each other and use it to improve'.	Feedback regarding pupils was characterised 'by 2 or 3 minutes quick chat to talk about what they did, what they didn't get'. Teacher's feedback to TAs was general rather than being directive, that is, focusing on what children didn't understand, rather than what TAs were doing and what TAs needed to do.	No communication.
Real understanding of learning and stages (teaching skills)	TAs would have good prior knowledge about the children and their learning and be able to use this knowledge to differentiate and adapt the material sufficiently within the learning outcomes if required to do so.	The TA had some knowledge and was still making a positive difference in classroom.	Lack of TA understanding resulted in pupils suffering in that pupils' learning was not being moved on.

Case study 3.2: Imaginary dialogue between SENCos discussing the use of 'model of collaboration'

Setting the scene: A group of SENCos were attending a training session as part of the National Award for SENCo Co-ordination and discussing some of the implications of the proposed model.

Joe: Well, it is an interesting model but not many of the teachers/TAs in our school are at the great/outstanding stage. I see that level in terms of trust, planning and feedback as something to aspire to. I think most of the teacher/TA relationships are at the average stage.

Dianne: I don't know about your school, but finding planning time is not easy. In terms of feedback . . . a two to three minute chat in the corridor or at the back of the classroom is about the best you can hope for, and if the conversation is concise and constructive it can be sufficient.

Zoe: I think it all goes back to time, resources and, of course, there is pay. Sometimes I feel we are giving TAs too much responsibility for the amount of money we are paying them.

Sandra: In terms of planning with TAs – well there are practicalities – our TAs/HLTAs are there in the class to cover when we are out planning.

Mike: I think a discussion on the involvement of TAs in planning is important. I think the role of the TA is to act under the guidance of a teacher – I don't ask them, I tell them what we are doing and, if they have an idea I will incorporate it, but that rarely happens.

Joe: Not all TAs would be interested in being involved in planning. And of course our planning happens after school and then we would be asking them to attend the planning meetings without being able to pay them.

Zoe: TA involvement in planning is interesting but I don't think all of the teachers in our school would be for it. Some, I think, would feel threatened, some would find it liberating and empowering and some would feel both.

Beth: I think having TAs involved in planning has made an incredible amount of difference to our school. We ask them all to stay back for one afternoon each week after school and in return they can come in late one morning. Having the TAs involved in planning means that they really feel that they are a valued member of the school and, more importantly, they really understand the learning objectives. Of course, that means they are better able to support the pupils in the classroom.

Tanya: In our secondary school, we have designated TAs assigned to departments. One lesson a fortnight is given over to teachers or departments sitting down with TAs and planning. This involvement in planning has led to the TA really understanding the subject, the teacher's working style and getting a real sense of where the teacher is within the scheme of work. Before we did this, the LSAs would be given the scheme of work and you would rely on them to look at it, but of course if they did not have a really good understanding of the subject level then this was very difficult.

Discussion points

a.   What do you think of the proposed model (Table 3.1)?
b.   To what extent do you agree or disagree with the above comments (case study 3.2)?

The dialogue in case study 3.2 is imaginary, but the issues and questions that it raises are anything but. Indeed, the research and literature on support staff deployment highlights examples of good practice, including involvement of support staff in planning time and two-way dialogue to ensure the sharing of ideas.

Ways of moving forward

Though the model of collaboration presented in Table 3.1 portrays ways of classifying relationships, what is more interesting and constructive is to explore ways of developing relationships.

Playing to strengths and developing strengths

An important part of an ideal relationship involves recognising and acknowledging TAs' strengths and using these strengths to effectively support pupil learning. The teacher first needs to know what the TA is good at, and that they would not 'make a point of giving him/her things to do that he/she doesn't like or he/she's not skilled at' (Bentham 2011). An audit of teaching assistants' strengths and areas for development would need to be discussed during performance/professional reviews. However, sometimes the reality of working in a busy school presents the teacher with challenges on how to deploy teaching assistants effectively. For example, a secondary teacher may find that the teaching assistant/ LSA in a particular class is lacking in specific skills and understanding of the subject being taught, a situation that may arise as the result of a TA being asked to cover classes due to timetabling issues, exams and illness. This would require the teacher to be able to think on his or her feet in order to decide in what capacity a TA should be best deployed to maximise pupil learning. The ability to effectively deploy TAs needs to be part of a teacher's repertoire of skills, as the following quote illustrates:

> You may have a TA [in a maths class] who is actually innumerate but has very strong English strengths, and so I would probably put her or him in a position where I could quickly correct any misconceptions but perhaps get them to work in a more collaborative way with better, more secure students in the room, perhaps closer to any who had behavioural problems so if the mathematical understanding simply wasn't there then I'd have to try to use them as best I could.

> (Bentham 2011)

In recognition that TAs have varying strengths, levels of experience and expertise, the degree of guidance and direction given to TAs must be flexible or 'fluid' to account for this variation. A teacher can slowly build on skills working within the TA's existing abilities. In recognising TAs' abilities, one teacher stated:

I'd rather she had fewer children [to help, and] done it well . . . equally with time, I think if I put pressure on her for time I think that's when I think things would become slapdash.

. . . I'll say to her 'I'm looking for quality', so I make her life easier and I think I should do.

(Bentham 2011)

Role models and observational learning

In learning how to effectively support pupil learning, TAs can observe the teachers they are working with and, therefore, teachers can be powerful role models. To maximise the potential of observational learning, TAs' personalities and skill sets can be matched to teachers' personalities and expertise. This strategy of ensuring suitably appropriate role models can be pivotal in transforming teacher and TA relationships. As one teacher stated:

I think half the time it's the model that you set, if I were slapdash she'd be slapdash.

Sometimes it's just a change [that is needed] – putting them in with a different teacher . . . sometimes putting them with a strong teacher, who's a powerful role model. Or even just someone who's a little bit more relaxed or someone's who's very direct can make a difference.

(Bentham 2011)

Selective praise and appropriate direction can also be used to improve TA practice.

So you would praise something: 'That's absolutely brilliant, I wonder if you could replicate that with so-and-so next lesson,' or you might say 'I want you to really focus on that group of 4 or 5 girls who keep drifting off . . . keep them bubbly and give them a focus and . . . just bring them on.'

(Bentham 2011)

Developing knowledge and skills

Let us recall, at this moment, our imaginary story involving Ms Smythe and Josie in which the teaching assistant felt that she knew better what should be done and the teacher felt that Josie, the TA, did not comprehend the complexity of the learning situation. One possible reason for criticism from some TAs could be due to the fact that there may be a lack of time for communication about lesson plans and, as such, TAs may struggle to understand what the teachers are doing and why. Developing TA knowledge could be a way forward. Here, we are looking at how TAs come to learn to effectively support pupil learning and development in the classroom. One TA compared the 'just picking things up' approach to an approach whereby strategies used were understood in the context of reflection on knowledge of pupil learning and development.

The more I've trained the more knowledgeable I've become, the more I've wanted to learn, because some TAs are happy to have the plans and they've been doing the job for years and that's it, they know what to do and they do it instinctively because they've been doing it for years and they've seen it taught so they've kind of picked it up. . . . But others will actively seek that knowledge of why it's done that way. That's the difference I think, it's like OK I know it's done that way and I can deliver it that way, but why is it done that way? How is that going to benefit the children? Why do we do it that way? Is there a better way? Can I suggest a better way?

(Bentham 2011)

Referring back to our imaginary case study, perhaps the teacher needs to discuss with and explain to her TA why she is teaching in such a way, and in doing so to make reference to relevant teaching strategies and educational theories. Perhaps, if the teaching assistant understood what the teacher was trying to accomplish, the teacher and the teaching assistant would be able to have more constructive conversations regarding how to improve pupil outcomes.

The question for school leadership teams concerns what type of TA the school requires to support pupil learning. Does the school want a TA who will technically and competently deliver learning tasks, or does the school prefer a reflective practitioner? The answer to this question will have implications on the training that is delivered to TAs and the extent to which TAs are involved in discussions regarding pupil learning.

Training sessions

Teaching assistants need skills and knowledge to effectively carry out their roles and responsibilities. To develop these prerequisite skills, teachers and senior management teams need to consider TA involvement in training. One teacher commented that his school thought carefully about how to involve their TAs:

We invite them in, if we think it's something that they might not be interested in . . . we give them tasks that are linked to it so that they can see there's a reason for it, for example when we were doing (training on) assessment for learning, we asked them to go and look through all the pupils' books that they'd worked with and see if they could find . . . good feedback to children and why they liked it so that . . . we could devise a way that they could feedback with the teacher.

(Bentham 2011)

Often, TAs mentioned the need for joint workshops about how teachers and teaching assistants should work together:

A lot of teachers don't know how or what the TA is there for so maybe some joint workshops for the teachers and the TAs you know it goes both ways, maybe the TA doesn't know what is expected of them but maybe the teacher doesn't know what they should expect of the TA.

(Bentham 2011)

Case study 3.3: Managing collaboration

In my role as an inclusion manager, I am responsible for 20 teaching assistants. Every month I have a meeting with the TAs to discuss relevant issues. What became apparent to me in these meetings was the confusion experienced by TAs when asked to work with different teachers. The TAs felt that different teachers had their own unique ways of working and likewise their own unique views regarding what they expected of the TAs in their classroom. TAs talked of not knowing what the right response was. Likewise, I have teachers coming to me and saying that they felt drained by a teaching assistant always comparing what they do to other teachers – phrases such as 'Miss so and so would do this' or 'Miss so and so would never do that'. In order to rectify this issue, I now have devised a form that both teacher and teaching assistant have to fill out at the beginning of each academic year. There are all sorts of questions on this form: what kind of behaviour support the teacher requires because different teachers prefer different levels of support; the type of admin support required; the type of feedback to be given to parents; who you would like them to be responsible for hearing read; timetables, etc. We have had this form in place for a year and for some teachers and teaching assistants it has made a positive difference to their relationship. Of course, I ask for a copy of form to be handed in to myself, and I can always tell those that have just gone through the motions and have written as little as possible. For the forthcoming year I am holding a joint inset day for both teachers and teaching assistants to go over the form, to amend the form if they feel it is necessary, and to give some examples of good practice.

Discussion points

How would you devise this form?

Case study 3.4: Feeding back from inset

Jocasta (TA): I just want to thank you for sending me on the course, and I know how expensive it was. I would just like to say how much I have benefited from going on the EAL course. I have learnt many really useful strategies for the classroom.

Jason (SENCo): And I trust you are now using these strategies. Have you seen a difference with the pupils you work with in the classroom?

Jocasta (TA): Well . . .

Jason (SENCo): It always takes time for strategies to have an impact.

Jocasta (TA): That's not it. I want to put these strategies into place and I think they would be really effective . . . but you know Mrs Jones. She is very firm on what we do in the classroom. As she says, 'I have been working with students for 20 years and I know what works and doesn't work.'

Jason (SENCo): Yes I see . . . I will talk to Mrs Jones.

Although this is an imaginary case study, it does highlight the difficulties teaching assistants have in implementing new ideas and strategies that have been gleaned from inset/training sessions. TAs will often talk of not being in a position of power or authority to make changes.

Discussion points

If you were the SENCo what would you say?

Critical incident theory

Critical incidents have been proposed as a way in which teachers and teaching assistants can become engaged in reflection on the nature of their working relationships. Critical incidents are brief descriptions of meaningful events (Brookfield 1995). These critical incidents are not necessarily dramatic events but are given importance, significance and meaning through personal reflection (Tripp 1993). Elliot (2010) sees critical incidents as ways of facilitating collaborative relationships through sparking discussions in order to raise awareness, challenge entrenched views, change practice and create greater platforms for understanding.

The following critical incidents were the outcomes of research conducted by Bentham (2011).

Critical incident 1: What makes for a collaborative working relationship? Is it subjective perceptions or impact on pupils?

In the following critical incident, a teacher reflects on how conducting one teacher observation transformed her views on teacher/TA relationships. To set the scene, the teacher was observing another teacher as part of a teacher's performance management process and knew from previous comments that the TA/teacher relationship being observed was described in glowing terms by both parties.

Critical incident 1

Sometimes teachers/TA teams can work in a completely, I would say adequate, happy way, they're happy, their TA is happy, the teacher is happy. I never thought there would be a problem until interestingly enough a teacher who had sung the praises of a TA all the time I'd been there, I had never worked with this TA and I went up to do an observation on the teacher, and this TA did absolutely nothing. She sat very quietly and she went 'uh huh', smiled at the children, nodded, pointed to things, but didn't actually do anything. And I worked out that that's why the teacher thought it was great because she likes to be in control.

Case study 3.5: Imaginary dialogue between SENCos discussing the critical incident – 'what makes for a collaborative relationship?'

Setting the scene: A group of SENCos were attending a training session as part of the National Award for SENCo Co-ordination.

Jane: Perhaps the teacher conducting the observation is being somewhat harsh. She is saying that the TA was smiling and nodding at the pupils and those non-verbal types of communication are important. Perhaps those smiles and nods were being used effectively to keep the pupils on task and giving the pupils the confidence to participate.

Sidney: Possibly, but maybe her point is that the TA is not being deployed as effectively as she could be. Maybe her skills and expertise could be used more appropriately or maybe the TA lacks the confidence to take a more active role in the classroom; perhaps she needs more training.

Sarah: But it is interesting that both the teacher and the TA thought they had a great relationship – that just shows that what is a great relationship is very much down to personal subjective feelings.

Sidney: A good or outstanding teacher/TA relationship must always be judged in terms of the impact it has on pupils' learning. That teacher and TA just seemed to be too comfortable. I wonder how long they had been working together. But, going back to your point about good relationships being subjective: that is really important. Perhaps there is no one ideal way of working but many – and it doesn't matter how you get there, so to speak, but the impact must be the same; that is, the impact of the relationship must always result in improvement in pupil learning.

Jane: I must admit that I tend to rely on what teachers and teaching assistants say – no news is good news – and I have built up a level of trust with my team over many years, so that I know if there were issues they would tell me. But it does make you think.

Sarah: Perhaps having discussions with teachers and teaching assistants about what they think a productive relationship looks like could be illuminating.

Discussion points

a. What is your opinion of the critical incident?
b. To what extent do you agree or disagree with the above comments?

Critical incident 2 (TA perspective): What more involvement in planning would mean to me

Critical incident 2 describes a situation in which a TA is supporting pupils on a topic involving 'famous pilots' from the First World War. The TA reflects that, though she had the plans in advance, there would be advantages to being both more involved in the planning and in having additional time to think and develop further knowledge on the topic.

Critical incident 2

At the moment we're doing a topic on the First World War. I honestly don't know a lot about the First World War; it would be nice to be able to have that time to go away myself and find out information. Because when the children ask you a question you think, well, actually I don't know, and sometimes you have to say 'I don't know, let's find out together', which is fine, but for me I just think it would be nicer to have that time to find out more. The teachers, they know what they're doing because it's in their heads already, they've discussed it. I do get the plans a week in advance but it would be helpful to have more time to think and prepare for the topic. It would be great if I was more involved in the planning.

Case study 3.6: Imaginary dialogue between SENCos discussing 'what more involvement in planning would mean to me'

Setting the scene: A group of SENCos were attending a training session as part of the National Award for SENCo Co-ordination.

Jolene: From my perspective, the TA is doing what she is supposed to. The strategy of saying 'I don't know and let's find out together' is a really effective strategy for encouraging independent learning.

Sadie: I think the TA is aware that it is an appropriate and effective strategy but that she feels she would be able to support the pupil's learning more if she had more underpinning knowledge herself.

Sam: From the perspective of a teacher, having that underpinning knowledge of a topic does allow you to support pupils' learning more effectively, in that you can more effectively question pupils and scaffold or develop their answers.

Jolene: But don't you think you would be expecting too much of a TA? She says she has the plans a week in advance, and that is good practice, but is it enough time?

Sadie: What would you do if your team of TAs said that they felt that they would be better able to support pupils if they were involved in planning meetings?

Jolene: Something to think about?

Though this dialogue is imaginary it does highlights important issues regarding teaching assistants underpinning knowledge of the subject material, suitable strategies to support learning and TA involvement in planning.

Discussion points

a. What is your opinion of the critical incident?
b. To what extent do you agree or disagree with the above comments?

Critical incident 3: The need for constructive feedback, or 'I can't always say what I think'

What follows is not one critical incident but several based around the theme of constructive feedback and the difficulty in saying things that need to be said in a manner that is understood, while also being mindful of not wanting to upset colleagues and respectful of positions of authority.

A TA's viewpoint

TA: If I'm going to take over your class in the afternoon, you would tell me if I was doing it wrong?

Teacher: Absolutely. I probably wouldn't tell you in terms like that, though.

TA: So how would I know, then, if you're not just being kind?

Teacher: Because I'm going to tell you and I'll give honest feedback and if you'd like me to I'm happy to.

TA: Because I don't want to let you down, I don't want to let the children down.

Teacher: That's absolutely fine, so if you want to ask me a direct question, I'll tell you what I think.

A teacher's viewpoint

Teacher: I can't always say what I think. My TA is quite happy about speaking her mind in a nice way, and I . . . I equally do that, but I do it in a much more considered or slightly manipulative way, but a nice manipulative way. If there is something I'm not happy about I'll twist it round so it's like I've done it or someone else has done it; therefore it's a win/win situation for everyone involved.

A TA's viewpoint

TA: It's how you come across to them, I mean if you go in where angels fear to tread and just say 'Look, you haven't seen that this child needs this' then it's rude and disrespectful. Teachers have done a lot of training, so if I did approach her I'd say 'Can I just make a suggestion?' However, there are some situations, often with new teachers, where I find I'm biting my tongue a lot, I'm sitting there thinking 'Just stop talking and wait for him to be quiet and then continue.'

Case study 3.7: Imaginary dialogue between SENCos discussing 'the need for constructive feedback'

Setting the scene: A group of SENCos were attending a training session as part of the National Award for SENCo Co-ordination.

Jolene: I can really relate to the teacher when she is saying that she is ever so slightly manipulative in how she communicates with the TA. Perhaps it is not about being direct, but it is about being considered in what you say and how tactfully you say it.

Shelby: I agree. I had this TA once who was extremely easy to upset, in fact, communicating with her was like walking on egg shells.

Jamie: Of course you have to be just really appreciative of the fact that the TAs are there doing all the work they do, especially when you consider just how little they are getting paid. Schools rightly need to be very grateful.

Sidney: I was talking to my team of TAs and what they appreciated and needed was really direct, constructive feedback. I know that I always try to be tactful but possibly, in being kind, nice and tactful, you are not actually getting the message across and perhaps you are inadvertently just confusing the TAs with mixed messages. The bottom line is that we are all here for the pupils and if TA practice needs to change in order to support the pupils in a better manner then we have to give that feedback. As teachers, we receive direct constructive feedback.

Jamie: Of course, it works both ways as that final critical incident illustrated. I have several experienced TAs working with NQTs and it is difficult. The NQTs are feeling somewhat undermined by the very experienced TAs and the TAs are coming to me saying that they are really struggling not to intervene, say something to the teacher or in some situations wanting to take control of the class. Not easy collaborating, is it?

Jane: Mutual constructive feedback is important, but when can this take place? At best, the teachers and TAs in our school have snatched conversations in corridors or a quick two or three minute chat at the back of the class before the next group of pupils arrive.

The dialogue between the SENCos is imaginary. However, the need for constructive feedback or joint dialogue, in which both teacher and TA would be able to take constructive criticism from each other and use it to improve, is seen as the ideal. For this to happen, training needs to focus on how these joint dialogues should be constructed and time needs to be found for these conversations.

Discussion points

a. What is your opinion of the critical incidents?
b. To what extent do you agree or disagree with the above comments?

Critical incident 4: What would trust look like in a collaborative relationship?

The following critical incident illustrates what a possible trusting relationship could look like, but acknowledges possible conflicts regarding what distinguishes a teacher from a teaching assistant.

TA: I've had a situation where a child emotionally broke down in a lesson after being told off by the teacher and I withdrew them from the class. I didn't ask the teacher – I just took them out. However, afterwards I thought, 'oh my goodness, the pupil has been in trouble with the teacher, the teacher has seen me take them out and the teacher is probably sitting there thinking 'Oh that's great. I've just dealt with that child and now you're giving them sympathy.' Anyway, after I calmed the pupil down we returned to the lesson, but I spent the rest of that lesson worrying that I'd overstepped my role. I went to the teacher afterwards and explained that I did at one point think maybe that they were really not happy with what I'd done. The teacher said 'Well at first I did think who's in charge in this class?' but she also said, 'I know you, and I know there would have been a good reason for you taking that child outside and I just went with it.' And for me that is what a trusting relationship is all about.

Case study 3.8: Imaginary dialogue between SENCos discussing 'what trust would look like in a collaborative relationship'

Setting the scene: A group of SENCos were attending a training session as part of the National Award for SENCo Co-ordination.

Sidney: My relationship with my TA is just like this – I trust her totally. But also we have spent time together establishing ground rules, so to speak. So in a situation where a child emotionally broke down in class I would expect her to take the pupil out and to deal with the situation as she saw fit.

Jolene: Ground rules are important. If I hadn't established a ground rule for this type of situation then I would see the TA as overstepping her role and I would wonder who is in charge of the classroom. And even if we did have ground rules I would still expect some non-verbal communication. The TA would look at me – look at the situation – look at me and I would nod or I would say something – if that makes sense. It all about how you work together.

Sam: I think this critical incident describes a teaching assistant who is very skilled – but not all teaching assistants would be working at this level. So the relationship a teacher and TA have in terms of responsibilities given to the TA is about trust but it is also about how skilled the TA is and how much guidance he or she requires.

Jody: Trust is important and it is important that a TA is highly skilled. Can you trust or give that amount of responsibility to act on their own initiative to a TA who is not highly skilled or is just developing their skills?

Sidney: I think trust means that you trust a TA to work within their existing skills and that when they are out of their depths, or the situation is such that it is not within their remit to deal with it, then you must trust them to hand the responsibility to you. The TAs I manage often talk in terms of trusting their teachers not to give them any task that they are not able to do.

Jane: In respect of the example in the critical incident, I would be happy with this situation but there are some teachers in my school who would not like this.

Jamie: This all goes back to how different teachers and TAs have different expectations and how what they see as an ideal relationship can differ. Of course, there needs to be some system in place where TAs and teachers can discuss expectations.

Sidney: But we need to remember that teachers and TAs need to move beyond a discussion of ownership and responsibility to a situation where each can work in mutual interdependence for the good of all children. Of course, the ownership and the responsibility for what happens within the classroom is the responsibility of the teacher; the role of the teacher is to guide and manage the TAs and the role of the SENCo is to guide and manage teachers and teaching assistants working together. Not easy!

Again, the discussion regarding the critical incident is imaginary but the issues it raises are anything but. There is debate regarding what a collaborative relationship should look like and it is ongoing. To move TA/teacher working relationships forwards there needs to be a whole school discussion of what an ideal collaborative relationship would entail, the necessary skills of the TA and the initial teacher training needed to realise this. Perhaps a discussion could take place in your school using the critical incidents and imaginary discussions presented in this chapter or, better still, these critical incidents could be used as a starting point for the creation and discussion of your own.

Teaching assistants are a valuable resource and, working together, teachers and TAs can accomplish more than either working individually. It is the hope that outstanding collaborative relationships will enable teachers and TAs to more effectively support pupil learning and to energise and direct – that is, motivate – each other and the pupils they work with.

Summary

In pulling together the information presented in these chapter teachers, TAs and schools need to consider:

- TA involvement in planning.
- How TAs are deployed and supported – for example, what levels of guidance a TA needs and how to determine this.
- Quality of mutual feedback; that is, how to say difficult things in a constructive manner.
- The importance of recognising and playing to TA strengths.
- Supporting teachers in their being an effective role model for the TAs.
- Developing TA knowledge and skills.

Chapter 4

Motivation issues for students – what pupils say

An overview

Then the whining school-boy, with his satchel
And shining morning face, creeping like snail
Unwillingly to school

(William Shakespeare, *As You Like It*, Act II, Scene vii)

Education is seen as perhaps the most valuable thing we can give our children. Yet it also seems that for centuries the actual act of going to school has had a bad press. Not only in Shakespeare's day, but also in modern popular music and culture, school is more often than not represented as a place of repression, unreality and irrelevance. Motivation for attending such an institution is likely to be largely lacking.

But what do those for whom school is provided say? This is the focus of this chapter. It seeks to deal with issues (both positive and negative) raised by pupils themselves regarding aspects of schooling which impact on their motivation to learn. Many of the comments expressed in this chapter are based on research conducted by Hutchins (2010). The comments from pupils will be linked with motivational and learning theory where appropriate. The voices of the pupils are not meant to be representative of all pupils, but they may be like pupils known to the readers of this book – or they may not. One aspect which we hope will come through is the variety of views and experiences held by pupils. Key to this chapter is the importance of listening to what pupils have to say – what is known in educational circles as 'pupil voice'. If we are to engage pupils in their learning, it is important to find out what pupils themselves think and feel about it, and the only way to do this is to ask them. 'Pupil voice' in research conducted by Hutchins (2010) was not found by giving children a questionnaire to fill out, nor sitting them down and asking them a range of predetermined structured questions; but it was rather providing them with an opportunity to discuss together what is important to them.

What pupils say: the role of the teacher

The way teachers treat, talk to, respond to and explain to pupils is vital in motivating them to engage with the lesson. Where pupils feel respected, listened to and taken seriously, they are more likely to respond positively both to the teacher and to the lesson, even if at times they are struggling to understand what to do.

How teachers help to motivate pupils

What the pupils say: Good old Mr Everest

A group of year 5 pupils talked about how one teacher in particular, Mr Everest, helped them learn:

Victoria: Mr Everest can make really boring lessons fun, and he also praises you for your work and doesn't say, 'that's rubbish'.

Edward: He's not like a normal teacher, he's a really excitable teacher 'cos he really helps us when we're stuck and then he actually pays attention to what we're saying.

Victoria: Some teachers don't do that. What Mr Everest does, if you're stuck on it he will give you an example and if you still don't get it, he won't talk to you like slowly like you're an idiot. He'll actually talk to you as in 'this is this and this is this' and then you'll get it. He actually speaks to you normally.

George: Mr Everest explains it very clearly. He uses words that we'd understand.

Albert: Mr Everest got really enthusiastic about the lesson, it was really cool. And *I* got enthusiastic about it as well.

Discussion points

a.   Identify as many different traits as possible of Mr Everest's teaching and personal qualities that are appreciated by the pupils.
b.   How do you make sense of these comments?

Teacher confidence in the pupils

Pupils know how a teacher feels about them – and that is highly significant when it comes to engagement and motivation. If teachers and teaching assistants are genuinely concerned for pupils, and express that concern in ways that pupils understand, then the pupils are more likely to be motivated to respond both to them and to the lessons.

Two year 6 pupils talk about how teachers can motivate pupils to learn:

Philip: When I gave some work in my teacher went 'I think you can do better.' They actually believe in you. Kind of not 'oghh, that's rubbish'.

Simon: Yeah, teachers have confidence in you. They give us *help* that's how some people know they've got confidence in us because they give us help.

Philip: Sometimes if the teachers *don't* have confidence in you, you go, 'Oh, what's the point of doing it. That teacher doesn't have confidence in me.' But if you do, then like, 'OK, I *can* do it. My teacher thinks I can do it.'

Discussion points

a. In what ways can a teacher or teaching assistant show they have confidence in pupils?
b. How do teachers or teaching assistants develop confidence in pupils when faced with challenging or demotivated pupils?

How teachers can demotivate pupils

But it is not all good news. Just as pupils see how teachers motivate them and encourage them to learn, other teachers can have the opposite effect. For example, demotivation from the perspective of the pupil can occur when teachers:

*   Are too strict.
*   Don't explain things well.
*   Expect too little, for example 'All we had to do was write *two* objects we would want to take to the rain forest. And it took her (the teacher) half an hour to explain. It was really boring. I just wanted to get on and *do* it.'
*   Don't understand the pupil, for example 'Say you were a very fidgety person and couldn't sit still. They move you because they think you're distracting people. I think a teacher should *know* the children and not tell you off for what you can't help.'
*   Don't appreciate that pupils have tried, for example 'You don't understand the piece of work but you did watch them and you're like "Miss, I need a bit of help". They'll be like "Oh, you didn't watch". Start blaming it on you. It's just sometimes the teachers can be unfair.'
*   Waste time, for example 'When people start talking in class, even though it's just a whisper, a little whisper, the teachers wait until everyone stops, and then it's like silence. Then for about two minutes, then they carry on and then someone does another little whisper and they wait again. And then they wait for a while and then they carry on again. The teachers are just wasting time, and it's really annoying. You just want to get on.'

Discussion points

a. Do you think these perceptions of the pupils are 'fair'? Why do you think that?
b. What could be done in the classroom to address some of these issues – if, indeed, any need addressing?

If the way teachers relate to pupils can affect pupil motivation, then *what* and *how* teachers teach is another way motivation can be affected.

Physical aspects of the lesson

A group of year 4 pupils, all of whom are achieving well in literacy, discuss aspects of lessons that they feel inhibit their learning:

What the pupils say:

Eric: I hate it 'cos there's too much writing.

Dawn: It's never creative enough, even though we could be writing our own stories, but we never do that it's just writing and reading, that's why I like art more because you have more freedom and you can express your feelings.

Eric: Art's OK, 'cos you don't have to do any writing or things.

Linda: Yeah, it doesn't make your hands hurt.

Dawn: It does if you paint loads and loads. But my hands do ache when we do nothing but write and write.

Linda: Sometimes I think my hand is going to drop off!

Eric: Mine goes a bit numb when I write too much.

Clearly, these pupils, even though they are 'good' at writing, sometimes found the actual act of writing difficult – it physically hurt them or, at least, made their hands ache. In a different conversation, pupils from other year groups (Hutchins 2010) said something similar about needing to put their hands up for long periods of time either to ask the teacher something or to respond to a teacher's questions. Keeping their hands raised for any length of time made their arms ache. You try it – they are right! Both groups of pupils are saying that their learning is hindered by being made to feel physically uncomfortable through what the teacher was asking them to do in a lesson.

The way school buildings and rooms are laid out and the facilities that a school has to offer can have a very real effect on pupil motivation. When a building is essentially in a mess the pupils get the idea that they themselves, and learning itself, are not very important. Pupils are helped to be motivated to learn by pleasant physical surroundings – that is obvious.

What the pupils say:

Bob: I don't like coming to school on Monday or Thursday because Mondays I'm always really tired, Thursdays I've got to get up early 'cos I have to go to Breakfast Club

Henry: [Talking about science lessons which took place at the end of the day] Science somehow gets you to feel really sleepy at the end. May be you could go outside and do science because you get fresh air and it's all stuffy inside for science.

Benjamin: Sometimes it can be a bit stressful. Sometimes if it's a really rainy day and the heating's on and all the windows are closed, you just feel really hot and you have to do this sum you can't work out, you just feel you want a break. You just want a refresh and *then* go back to school.

Pupils, unsurprisingly, are like their teachers and teaching assistants – getting up early and coming to school after the weekend can be difficult. What may be surprising is that they say how much this affects their learning. There is nothing anyone can do about Monday mornings – or any other morning for that matter – but it is worth bearing in mind that the pupils in your class may be responding poorly to work simply because they are tired or, as other pupils said, the room is too hot, too stuffy, too dark, too noisy or whatever. Heat in classrooms can be a real issue. It is sometimes worth going out of the classroom and coming back in after a minute or so simply to see how stuffy it gets with all the windows closed and thirty human beings sitting there, each one giving off heat. Getting those windows open can liven things up for the pupils, and for the teacher and teaching assistant.

Pace and content of the lesson

To be motivated to participate in a lesson and learn what the teacher is trying to teach, pupils must feel the lesson is worthwhile, that what they are being asked to do is neither too hard nor too easy and that it is presented in a way in which they can engage.

What the pupils say:

'When you find it challenging, but not really hard that you can't be bothered to do it.'
'More moving around in lessons and stuff would be better.'
'We wouldn't be sitting down like lemons; we could be actually getting up and doing something.'
'It has to be interesting, but you have to *learn* stuff. Science is really boring if they're *telling* you what to write.'
'I don't really like science but I like experiments. I remember Sir got these little rocket things, it was well awesome, put vinegar and something in it, powder I think. Then said see if it went *off*. The first time it didn't go off, but the second one we tried it and it went off and it went 'wooh', it went high in the sky.'

Discussion points

a.   Which lessons do your pupils find motivating?
b.   What are the factors within these lessons that promote their motivation to learn?

Extra-curricular activities

What goes on in a school outside of formal lessons can have a dramatic effect on pupils' motivation to learn. A group of year 4 pupils talk about this aspect of schooling.

What the pupils say:

Dawn: We've got lots of clubs – basketball club, netball club.
Eric: Karate.
Bob: And there's a lot of residential trips.
Eric: Yeah, lots of fun trips to places.

Going away as a group for a week, three days or even on a day trip does something to the cohesion of a group of pupils. It can promote the sense of belonging and participation that Wenger views as being essential aspects of communities of practice (see Chapter 1, pp. 15–16). Children who attend school clubs or go on school trips are more likely to see themselves as being 'part' of the school than if they did not have this opportunity.

The use of ICT

Children right across the primary phase of education seem to agree that ICT, the use of computers and other technology, motivates them to learn. One girl, who was otherwise very negative about school, stated 'ICT rules' and it 'rules', she says, 'because it is fun'.

'Fun' is a really important word for pupils in both the primary and the secondary sectors of education. 'Fun' does not mean it has to be funny or silly, nor does it mean the teacher and teaching assistant have to become some sort of entertainer. 'Fun' for these pupils means something they can get involved with, something that engages their attention, something they feel 'belongs' to them.

What the pupils say:

Claire: I think ICT's much more interesting 'cos you don't have to write stuff down. And you do a large variety not like in maths just sitting down just about all maths.

Katherine: I don't like writing; writing's my weakest point, unless it's on the computer – then I'm fine.

Peter: I like ICT. Well, who doesn't? Well, I'm very good with computers. I want to be a computer programmer when I grow up.

John: ICT, yeah *love* ICT. In ICT you find pictures of rainforests, that's what we done a few times and you like do some research, even though it sounds boring, it's actually quite fun. Yeah I just like ICT, it's fun. (Usually, John is very negative about every aspect of school. He is not motivated to learn. He does not see the point of it. He gets angry with himself and with others because he feels he is continually being forced to do something he does not want to do. Yet, when it comes to ICT, ICT is 'fun' and he enjoys it.)

Discussion points

a. Why do you think ICT is such a 'turn-on' for pupils?
b. In what ways could ICT be used to encourage pupil motivation to learn?
c. Do you see any pitfalls in using ICT in this way?

Emotional and psychological factors

No one would doubt that education is emotive. Emotions run high over all sorts of things – both for pupils and for teachers and teaching assistants. When considering how to help pupils be motivated to learn and to engage with their work, how they are responding emotionally must be taken into account.

What the pupils say:

Henry: Sometimes you don't get picked when you're the first one with your hand up and it's really annoying because if you're ready first and then the teacher picks someone else it's quite annoying.

Matilda: If you want to ask a question and there are loads of people with their hands up and people they pick have really silly questions and then you've got a really important question and that gets quite annoying because then you get stuck and get told off for not doing work.

Anne: They ask for questions to do with your work, but sometimes you think, 'I have a more important question than that', and so then you just sit down and wait until the teacher's finished, but sometimes when the teacher's finished they say, 'Now get your literacy books and go to your tables' and you're not allowed to get up and ask the teacher the question.

Discussion points

a.   In what ways might these pupils be demotivated by their experiences?
b.   In what ways, if any, could such emotions be alleviated in the classroom?
c.   How should the teacher or teaching assistant respond to them?

The behaviour of a few can affect the learning of the many

Pupils have a lot to say about poor behaviour and its effect on their learning.
    What the pupils say:

Sarah: If someone disrupts in class, they're being a bit ruder than they actually think. Some children in places don't get to go to school and they'd love it if they could go to school, and we just take it for granted.

Benjamin: In order to learn you have to *earn* it by respecting each other.

Mary: Shouldn't get into fights, shouldn't mess around in class, so you can learn like what you're *meant* to learn instead of being interrupted all the time.

Benjamin: Sometimes in lunch our class gets into lots of fights and we come in and then people start getting in a mood with each other because some people want to have a fight. Sometimes they barge into someone and they get angry and when you're trying to learn and the teacher has to stop and then it's just really annoying.

Simon: Sometimes I don't feel like going to school. Just in case I get bullied. I get bullied sometimes. People don't like school because they get *bullied*.

Philip: Some people in our class stop me learning.

Dan: Some people on me and Simon's table like talk and it's really hard to write.

Philip: Some people go off in a strop and then the teacher has to sort them out. That's affecting our education because *we're* like, missing out, just because of that one person.

Esther: Miss has two classes in one class. The front people are always the most well-behaved and then the back people just like, it's like the *good* people and the *bad* people. And that doesn't motivate you *at all*.

Case study 4.1: The behaviour of the few affects the learning of the many

Mr Smith's year 5 class are lining up in the playground to come in from lunchtime break. He leaves the staff room to go into the playground, stand at the front of the line and lead his class in. However, when he gets there he sees three boys pushing and shoving each other at the back of the line. One of them is crying, the other two are shouting angrily at each other. He stands at the front and tells them to be quiet and line up properly. They ignore him and carry on with their fight. Mr Smith raises his voice, still no effect. By this time many of the rest of the class are looking round to see what is happening and are beginning to chat together. Mr Smith goes to the back of the line. By now the three boys are hitting each other. One of the angry boys is becoming quite out of control and is lashing out with his fists. Mr Smith stands between this pupil and the other two to prevent anyone getting hurt. He speaks calmly to the boys saying that he will listen to their stories when they get into class and each one will have a chance to say what happened, but they need to calm down and walk into school quietly. If they do not calm down, he tells them, he will send them to the head teacher. Two of the boys grudgingly lower their voices and line up. A third continues to show anger and tries to hit the other two. Mr Smith tells him to go to the head teacher and, after swearing at the other pupils, he does so. Mr Smith is now able to lead his class into the school building. The incident has taken four minutes so far to bring to this resolution but, once back in the classroom, more of Mr Smith's time is taken up trying to sort out what happened and why these boys got into their fight.

Discussion points

a. What do you think pupils not involved in the fight thought while Mr Smith was trying to sort it out?
b. How would you summarise the impact on motivation and on learning by the poor behaviour of some of these pupils?
c. What do you think should be the response from the teacher or teaching assistant?
d. What would the pupils you work with say about the behaviour of others?

Extrinsic and intrinsic motivation

Schools are likely to have a system of rewards and sanctions. Rewards come in many forms and can be effective in enhancing motivation. The children below talk about achievement points which are given for good work, good effort and good behaviour. Achievement points result in the giving of certificates (bronze, silver, gold and platinum). The response of pupils to this reward is mixed, as can be seen from the following conversations between pupils in year 6.
     What the pupils say:

Sarah: That's what I do first thing. I check my work from the day before to see if I've got any achievement points and now I've got my silver certificate.

John: I don't put my achievement points up. Last year I didn't *do* so well in the achievement points. It just took *ages* and it just gets boring, I can't really be bothered.

Esther: To be honest, I do *care* about getting achievement points, but I'd rather get something else. I'd rather get a star to stick on a piece of work. I like stickers on my work if I've been good. Miss sent me down to the head teacher and I got a sticker, and it motivates me to do more.

Thomas: I *do* like achievement points, 'cos when I get the certificates, when you're like standing up there in assembly you feel quite good and then when you go home and your parents are pleased.

Ruth: But it is just a piece of paper at the end of the day. I'd rather work because I enjoy the work and I want to be good.

Linda: My report was really, really good 'cos I got really good levels and there was nothing saying bad things about me. My mum and dad were really pleased with me, so all day they said, 'Well done Linda, well done Linda for your report', and then for a surprise me and my sister got a laptop.

Dawn: My dad said he'd get me a treat for a good report and good parents' evening, but I don't know what to get.

Discussion points

a. In motivational theory, intrinsic motivation is usually regarded as being more effective than extrinsic motivation. Do these comments from the pupils bear this out, or do you think they challenge this view? Why? Can these comments be explained by reference to cognitive evaluation theory (p. 51) and forms of external regulation (p. 48)?

b. Do you think it is significant that only one pupil expressly stated she worked because she wanted her work to be good? Why do you think this? How does this relate to theories of fixed and growth mindsets (see pp. 58–60)?

c. In a recent television documentary, an inner city secondary school in the United States was shown to be motivating their students by giving them significant sums of money for good behaviour or good work. How do you think this relates to the comments made by the pupils above?

Self-perception

All of the learning theories considered in Chapter 1 and the theories of motivation looked at in Chapter 2 agree on one thing in particular – what happens to pupils in schools shapes how they see themselves. Technically known as 'learner identity', these children talk about how they see themselves in school. It is worth thinking about the reasons they give for the way that they talk about themselves in different subjects.

What the pupils say:

Bob: I think I'm good*ish* in maths because I was not that good and now I've moved up a level and now I'm good*ish*. I find maths quite easy but I don't like it.

Eric: I think I've done quite well 'cos I've improved a level in literacy, gone up to a new table. Not doing as well as that in maths though. I'm not sure if maths is really my thing.

Linda: I have a higher level in maths than middle set and the bottom set. Plus, I'm not *rubbish* at maths and I'm not extremely good at maths. I don't think I'm absolutely that good at maths because I'm not on the highest table. 'Cos green table's the highest, then I'm on red table.

John: I'd like to be somebody who is *really* good at something.

Matthew: I find quite a bit of work hard, but I find some aspects easy. I quite enjoy helping other people when they're stuck, and I feel as though I'm gradually moving *up* so I'm helping other people to go up as well.

Peter: I *think* without me misbehaving, which I find quite difficult, I think I'd do really, really well. I'm alright at school but I can't wait to get home at the end of the day. I believe in myself.

Simon: Don't feel confident because it's a bit hard. I like difficult work 'cos it helps me think, you know like help my brain, and I like working with like new stuff.

Esther: Loads of people in our class don't feel good about themselves and they haven't got self-confidence.

Dawn: Sometimes I'm a good learner, but sometimes I'm not.

Discussion points

a.   What 'learner identities' do these pupils have? Do they have learning goals or performance goals (refer to pp. 56–57)?

b.   How do you think they have gained these identities?

c.   What impact do you think their perceptions of themselves have on their motivation to learn? (Hint: you may wish to consider fixed and growth mindsets, pp. 58–60.)

What have these pupils told us?

At the very least, these pupils have told us that motivation is not a simple or straightforward issue. There is no single 'cause and effect' so that, if a teacher puts something in place, the pupils in the class will automatically be motivated to learn. Far from it. Motivation is a complex issue that is influenced by many things. Among these many factors, the pupils have emphasised the following:

The role of the teacher

The teacher is crucial. Teachers who care for the pupils as individuals and who show that concern through the way they talk with and listen to pupils are likely to help motivate children to learn. As one pupil put it, it's good to be 'an excitable teacher'. Teacher enthusiasm is contagious, but so is teacher boredom, disinterest and disengagement. Pupils need to know that their teachers have confidence in them. This ties in exactly with the 'self-fulfilling prophecies' (p. 44), the 'Self theories' of Carol Dweck (see pp. 58–60) and the principles behind effective Assessment for Learning (see Chapter 5) whereby, in order to provide an environment which encourages motivation to learn, teachers must believe that their pupils can increase in intelligence and ability (what Dweck terms holding an 'incremental' view of intelligence, or having a 'growth' mindset).

Physical issues

Physical aspects of the lesson also affect motivation and learning. Where pupils feel they are asked to write too much; to have their hands up in the air too long; to be made to sit on the carpet for extended periods of time; to have to sit still and listen rather than actively be engaged; and to be required to sit in enclosed stuffy, hot classrooms, motivation to learn is likely to be restricted. In one sense this is obvious, but it can be easily overlooked.

A sense of belonging

When the pupils spoke about after school clubs and school residential trips they were saying something about their sense of 'belonging' to the school. School is compulsory – the clubs and trips are voluntary. They are something the children *choose* to do, and choice is a crucial aspect of motivational theory. Wenger's 'communities of practice' (Chapter 1) come in here. The pupils who feel they 'belong' in the school are more likely to be motivated to learn than those who feel no such sense of identity with the school. For pupils, their involvement in the school trips was important because it was something they did 'outside' normal school. They related with other pupils and with teachers and teaching assistants in a different way – as one teacher commented, 'When they are in school, they are *pupils*; but when they are on residentials they are *children*.' This involvement in outside activities often resulted in there being more of a sense of 'togetherness' when they came back into school for normal lessons.

ICT

Using ICT seems to give pupils a sense of choice and control. Even where they are using this technology to do 'normal' school work like writing, their motivation to learn is greater than when using more traditional methods. Choice is something very important in all motivational theories – it is called pupil 'agency' (see Chapter 1). Where pupils feel some measure of control and choice over what they do they are more likely to be motivated to learn. (For a further discussion on choice and control see pp. 52, 61.)

Challenging behaviour

How pupils behave has a major impact on motivation to learn; for example, one pupil's fear of being bullied limited his ability to focus on his learning. Other pupils wanted to get on with their learning but were prevented from doing so by the disruption caused to the class by poor behaviour. Teacher response to poor behaviour is also an important factor from the pupils' perspectives. The way teachers deal with challenging behaviour and the amount of time they take on this is seen by many to be harmful to their own learning. When commenting on this, pupils seem to be saying they resent both the way the teachers respond to inappropriate behaviour and the fact that other pupils force them to do this by their poor behaviour.

Extrinsic and intrinsic motivation

The difference in views expressed by pupils confirms what many motivational theorists argue – there is no straightforward 'right or wrong' about extrinsic or intrinsic motivation. In its starkest form, extrinsic motivation is seen as something purely external to the pupil – a reward for responding 'correctly' or a sanction for responding 'incorrectly'. But what the pupils are saying is something more than this. The extrinsic 'reward' of achievement points or being given a sticker by the head teacher holds *value* for some pupils. The *extrinsic* reward is effective in boosting motivation to learn because it connects in some way with the child's *internal* workings – their mind, will, and emotions. The relationship between intrinsic and extrinsic rewards are complex, as discussed in cognitive evaluation theory (p. 51), where it is not the reward being given that is important but the *meaning* placed on that reward by the person receiving it that matters.

Whilst it may be the case that *intrinsic* motivation – the desire and willingness to work at learning for its own sake – is inherently 'better' than pure extrinsic motivation, very few children (and adults for that matter) function in that way. We all like to be recognised and rewarded for our attitude, work and effort – and most pupils do too. Those who said they did not care about these sorts of rewards did so because they were either disengaged with the whole of schooling, and felt that no matter what they did they would never succeed, or they were disengaged from the school's reward system because their work was so good and they were so confident in their abilities that they felt they did not need the rewards.

Education and culture

Bruner's theory of learning as culture (see Chapter 1) is borne out by many of the pupils who talked positively about the reward systems in the school. Those who appreciated certificates did so because it pleased their parents. A good report and high levels were praised and rewarded very tangibly at home. For these pupils, the culture of the school was reinforced by the culture of the home. The two coincided and the one had a positive effect on the other – school success was rewarded at home, which encouraged the pupils to strive for even greater success in school. These pupils identified with school and with the learning at school; therefore they were motivated to learn. It made sense to them. It connected with their experiences outside school.

Motivation and giftedness

Whilst this book is not about 'gifted' children, there is a good deal written about giftedness in pupils which has to do with motivation and therefore has a bearing on what this book *is* about. Some consideration is given to this aspect of motivation in this section, but what is written about motivation and gifted pupils can apply to any and all pupils.

'Gifted' pupils, according to national policy in England, are pupils who are performing within the top 10 per cent of their class in certain subjects, mainly English and/or maths. It is often thought that one aspect of 'giftedness' or simply relatively 'high achievement' is motivation – the more motivated a pupil is the more likely he is to achieve, and the more highly a pupil achieves, the more likely he is to be motivated. However, a large number of researchers over many years and in various countries have found that the situation is far more complex than this. Some of the findings of these researchers are presented below in order to provide a context for teachers and teaching assistants to reflect on their own perspectives and practices on how to motivate pupils to learn.

Persson (1998) reported that teachers commonly use personality traits of pupils such as being 'well motivated' to identify pupils as being 'gifted'. Such children seem to be 'talented for schooling' (p. 182). Joan Freeman (1998) also found that high levels of motivation were regarded as a mark of giftedness, but such children could be demotivated by the learning environment of the classroom: 'A child with a speedy and curious mind can suffer from boredom in an undifferentiated classroom' (p. 38). A gifted pupil can quickly become bored if they are presented with work they do not find interesting or challenging. Teachers, if they are not careful, can easily teach to the 'middle' of the class, where the majority of the class are. Those whose learning is at a higher level than the majority can miss out, as can be seen in this next case study.

Case study 4.2: James the gifted mathematician

James is in a year 4 maths class. The aim of the lesson is to learn to add hundreds, tens and units in columns. The teacher has put an example on the flipchart:

$$452$$
$$+ \ 137$$

James knows the answer immediately and puts his hand up to give his response. He is the first pupil to do so. The teacher waits for more pupils to raise their hands, and then he chooses someone else.

As most pupils take a longer time to respond, the teacher says, 'We will do some more examples of this so that you all have a chance to practice this method.' He writes up five more sums of similar difficulty. James is bored because he knows the answers to all of them as soon as they are written up. He does not need to write the answers down; he can do it in his head. He soon starts thinking about what he is going to be doing after school and 'tunes out' what is happening around him.

In this scenario the teacher is taking no account of James's ability and prior knowledge. He is so focused on the fact that the majority of his class still need to learn this addition method that he loses sight of the fact that he has one pupil whose learning is in advance of the others.

James – a gifted mathematician – is bored. He is losing interest and losing motivation.

Setting challenging work is important for gifted pupil, but it is easy to assume that gifted pupils will always be motivated if their learning is being stretched. However, a study by Boaler (Boaler 1997; Boaler et al. 2000) investigated gifted pupils in a top maths set in a secondary school and found the situation to be more complex than this. She found that many of the girls in particular had lost motivation to learn because the lessons, although 'stretching', were *too* stretching. The girls told her that they were demotivated in maths because they felt the teacher viewed them as being 'able' and therefore as being able to keep up with the fast pace of his teaching. This had become a real pressure to them. Motivation is a real balancing act – not being bored on the one hand because it is all too easy and not being crushed on the other hand because it is too difficult.

Over the years, Robert Sternberg in the USA has developed several models of giftedness ('Successful Intelligence', giftedness as 'Developing Expertise' and 'WICS – Wisdom, Intelligence, Creativity, Synthesised') which have major implications for schools. In all of these models of intelligence, motivation is key to developing any kind of expertise: 'Motivation is perhaps the indispensable element needed for school success; without it, the student never even tries to learn' (Sternberg 2001, p. 164). Phillips and Lindsay (2006) agree. They argue that 'Motivation could be regarded as the vital '*x* factor' in high levels of performance and achievement' (p. 58). Challenge is an important factor in promoting learning as motivation – if tasks are not challenging enough for pupils, their need for achievement will not be satisfied and so their learning stifled. This can be seen in the case of James in his maths lesson. A learning environment which promotes motivation should include a place where pupils experience genuine choice about the content and nature of their learning, where they exercise a good deal of independence in the learning process and where they are able to explore their own interests rather than being restricted all the time by what the curriculum says they have to learn.

An alternative approach to the maths lesson in which James got bored could promote rather than restrict his interest and motivation:

Case Study 4.3: James – a good lesson

James is in a year 4 maths class. The aim of the lesson is to learn to add hundreds, tens and units in columns. The teacher has put an example on the flipchart:

$$\begin{array}{r} 452 \\ + \ 137 \end{array}$$

Rather than ask pupils to put their hands up when they have worked out the answer, the teacher has given each member of the class an individual whiteboard and pen. He asks them to write out the question and then answer it, but he also says that those children who can do it in their heads need only write the answer. He asks that pupils raise their whiteboards so he can see their answers as soon as they have completed the answer. In this way he knows immediately that James has grasped the aim of the lesson. The teacher tells James that his answer is correct and congratulates him on how fast he responded. He then says

> If you have understood this question, it is time to move on to adding up hundreds, tens and units carrying across the columns. I have here some worksheets with those sorts of questions on. If you think you are ready to move on to this, come and collect them, go back to your tables and begin working on them. If you think you need more practice on adding without carrying, stay on the carpet and we'll go through some more.

James immediately picks up a worksheet, returns to his table and sets to work on something more challenging. He finds the first few questions easy, but then discovers the teacher has slipped in questions relating to thousands as well as hundreds, tens and units and has then also included working to one decimal place. James is thrilled and actually begins to sway from side to side as he works, almost as though he was listening to music.

What is happening here?

James's need both for choice and for challenge has been met; consequently his motivation to learn is maintained and even strengthened. His intrinsic enjoyment in maths is evident for all to see.

Discussion points

How do you think this short discussion on motivation and giftedness could influence what you do in the classroom?

Peer influence

'You're a bit of a swot aren't you?'

'Look out, here comes brain box!'

Most pupils want to be liked and to 'fit in' with their peers. Comments of ridicule like these could easily be made about those pupils who work hard and achieve high marks, especially by those who do not engage with school. In such instances, you would think that the pupils who were the subject of such ridicule would limit their motivation to learn in order to conform to the general ethos of their peers. Peer influence is often regarded in this negative way. In fact, research (Smith et al. 2005) found something quite different to this commonly-held perception of peer influence.

Their report found that most pupils who were high achievers and who showed good levels of motivation to work were not ridiculed. They were not made to feel strange or different by their peers. In fact, they were often looked up to. What made some pupils the subject of snide comments and jeers was the way these pupils were seen to behave. If they were viewed as behaving a lot differently from the norm, *then* they were often made the subject of jokes and teasing. So, it was not so much their motivation or their learning but perceived strange behaviour that made them stand out from the crowd.

Making sense of what pupils say by looking at what some motivation theorists say

Wynne Harlen

Wynne Harlen (2006) summarises various aspects of school as being crucial for motivating pupils:

- The subject needs to engage the pupils' interest.
- Pupils need to be encouraged to engage in 'mastery' or 'work' goals (where the focus is on the process of gaining knowledge) rather than 'performance goals' (where the focus is on demonstrating ability, getting good grades and out-performing other pupils). This is developed further in Chapter 2, pp. 56–57.
- Pupils need to have a sense of control over their learning, i.e. learning is something they do rather than something that simply happens to them. To develop such a sense of control pupils need to view success or failure as being down to their own effort and hard work rather than some innate, fixed ability or to circumstances outside their control, such as whether a particular test was 'hard' or 'easy'. This links with attribution theory (pp. 34–36) and fixed and growth mindsets (pp. 58–60).
- Schools need to teach pupils how to fail, in order for pupils to develop a sense of identity as learners. Pupils' sense of 'self', needs to be strong enough to respond positively to setbacks. 'Self' includes self-esteem (how they value themselves as people and as learners), self-efficacy (how capable the pupil feels at learning a particular subject) and self-regulation (a pupil's willingness to act in ways that bring about learning). This is developed more fully in Chapter 2, pp. 61–62.

Alan McLean

McLean (2009) argues that 'pupils' motivation is easily malleable' (p. 5) – it is like soft clay which can be shaped, rather than fired clay which is hard and whose shape has become fixed.

This is not to say that it is easy for teachers or teaching assistants to motivate pupils to learn. It is simply to say that motivation is not a static, once-and-for-all thing. However, experience in schools tells us that it is easier for highly motivated pupils to lose their motivation (although this can take some doing) rather than to motivate pupils who have become thoroughly demotivated and disengaged.

'Engagement' is a key phrase for McLean, whereby engaged pupils take control over their learning and use their initiative. Disengaged learners, on the other hand, are essentially passive when it comes to learning or, more seriously, actively resist the process of learning.

The three As

He develops what he calls the 'three As' of motivation:

- *Affiliation* – the need to feel a sense of belonging.
- *Agency* – the need to feel that you can meet the demands of the task.
- *Autonomy* – the need to be self-determining, i.e. to be able to decide for yourself what you need to do to complete a task.

He believes that 'pupils with high satisfaction levels of affiliation, agency and autonomy will have high motivation to learn, and those with low satisfaction will have low motivation' (p. 16).

To some extent, 'affiliation' corresponds to Wenger's 'participation in a community of practice' (see pp. 15–16). Pupils who feel they belong in the class can identify with the values and routines of the class and are likely to be motivated to respond positively to learning. Pupils who feel they belong in the class are likely to have friends there, rather than those pupils who feel outside of the class or even alienated from it. A key aspect of the development of such a sense of belonging is the relationship between teacher, teaching assistant, and pupil. Think back to the case studies about James, the gifted mathematician. In the first case study, James is likely to feel on the outside of the class if his experiences of being bored become commonplace but, by the teacher responding and planning differently, James, in the second case study, clearly enjoys learning and feels a sense of belonging even though he is doing something different to the majority of the other pupils. In fact, he feels he belongs precisely *because* he has been given something different to do. As McLean writes, 'Pupils who feel appreciated and supported by their teachers feel positive about school, and this feeling is not just a by-product but a core ingredient of their engagement' (p. 18).

Case Study 4.4: Being flexible

It is the start of the school day in a year 4 class. The whole school is engaged in a week's focus on sport – learning about sports and sports personalities, writing about sport, investigating sports questions in maths and pupils participating in sports themselves. This morning the class teacher (Miss Entwistle) has organised the initial whole-class activity around the creation of imaginary new sports from the joining of two existing sports. On the interactive whiteboard she has already written 'foot-minton' which she describes to the class as a combination of football and badminton. The class discuss this for a bit, then she asks them to work in groups at their tables to come up with imaginary sports of their own. As the class settle to this, Miss Entwistle goes round the room talking to pupils directly about the activity.

Over the course of ten minutes there is continuous personal interaction between Miss Entwistle and the pupils – either individually, in groups or with the class as a whole. After this period of time she asks the class to stop their work and to share their ideas. She uses humour and jovial rapport a great deal. One pupil shares her idea of 'ten-diving', which she explains is playing tennis whilst sky-diving. Several of the pupils begin to laugh at this pupil, who often comes out with responses which could be described as being 'outside the box'. The teacher, however, takes this pupil and her responses seriously and, after thanking her for her contribution, she begins a short discussion with the class about gravity, asking them which would reach the ground first, a tennis ball or a sky-diver?

In this class, Miss Entwistle has created a good level of engagement with her pupils. She likes them, respects them and takes them seriously, but is also able to share a joke with them. She has a relaxed, yet very organised approach to learning. The class respond very positively to her and to her teaching. In McLean's terms, Miss Entwistle has made her class feel appreciated and supported by her. She is also able to teach in a flexible way – changing and developing her teaching and interaction with pupils as she goes along. For McLean, teacher flexibility is possibly *the* fundamentally crucial factor in promoting pupil motivation. The teacher must be aware of how her pupils are responding to what is being taught and be flexible enough to change both what and, perhaps more especially, how it is being taught. He writes, 'The motivating teacher gains influence by demonstrating an ability to adjust to the needs of pupils' (p. 6) – which is exactly what Miss Entwistle was doing. This ties in very closely to the concept of Assessment for Learning helping to promote motivation, as discussed in Chapter 5.

Learning stances

Building on McLean's argument, teaching in the classroom can be like sailing a yacht in the sea. The yacht is moving through the water on a course, but the water is itself moving underneath the boat in a way that cannot be directly sensed by the skipper of the yacht – all she sees is water, she cannot see that there are currents and tides pushing the sea in all sorts of directions. If these movements of water are not taken into account, the boat will end up in a very different place from that planned. What McLean terms the 'learning stances' of the pupils in the class can be likened to these tides and currents lurking unseen under the boat's hull. Some of these tides and currents may be conflicting with each other and may be heading in a totally different direction to the boat. These 'currents' can be influenced by many factors, all of which remain hidden to the teacher or teaching assistant. The child's family situation, how well or ill the child feels, whether or not a pet has recently died or a relationship has split up are some factors among many which can adversely affect the pupil's motivation to learn on any particular day. To get to where she wants to get to, the teacher must be as aware as possible of these currents, take them into account, and adjust her teaching accordingly, just as a competent helmsman will adjust the course of the boat to take the tides and currents into account. Just as to stick determinedly to a set course is to court disaster, so to continue teaching rigidly and inflexibly is to invite pupil demotivation and even alienation.

A common mistake that teachers make, McLean goes on to argue, is to view motivation as something residing just within the pupil – as being an inherent part of their make-up which they can do little about. Motivation is more complex: 'Motivation is not a feature of the learner but of the transaction between the learner and the context. Motivation, like trust, occurs between people rather than within people' (p. 8). To be a motivating teacher, McLean argues, requires confidence that what you do as a teacher matters – it can and will often, although not always, change the way a pupil responds to learning.

Teacher motivation

Because the role of the teacher is so crucial, McLean states that 'any discussion about pupil motivation must start with the conditions that affect teachers' motivation. You cannot share what you do not have; pupil autonomy can only flourish in a culture of teacher autonomy' (p. 231). For example, if you as a teacher or teaching assistant are demoralised, for whatever reason, it is very difficult to find the energy and motivation yourself to inspire motivation in your pupils. For Mclean, the three As apply just as much to teachers as to pupils. In order to motivate pupils to learn, teachers (and teaching assistants) need to have their own need for affiliation, agency and autonomy met. They too need to feel a sense of belonging, to feel that they can meet the demands of the task, and to feel that they are, to a large extent, in control of what they do.

Dale Schunk, Paul Pintrich and Judith Meece

Schunk et al. (2010) also place high importance on the role of the teacher in promoting motivation. For them, 'learner identity' – how pupils see themselves as learners – is a crucial factor in motivation. If pupils see themselves as being capable learners who can make a difference to their learning (self-efficacy) they are more likely to be motivated to learn than if they feel that whatever they do will not change their experience of learning. A sense of failure, especially failure that they can do nothing about, is an extremely strong *de*motivating experience. But how pupils see themselves does not happen automatically; it is built through experience and encounters with others. Teachers who lack confidence in their ability to help students learn may 'dwell on negative images about their classrooms' whereas 'those with greater confidence are apt to think of their students as motivated to learn' (p. 141). These different teachers are likely to react in different ways to their students, and from those reactions students' own sense of learner identity is going to be shaped.

Case study 4.5: How teachers' attitudes shape learner identity

Two secondary teachers are snatching a few minutes in the staffroom during break time. One teaches geography, the other English, and the day before they both had the same year 9 class to teach:

Geoffrey (to Belinda): What a nightmare 9F was! I couldn't get through to them at all. They were so unruly.

> *Geoffrey (thinking to himself):* Actually I feel a bit scared of some of them. I do not feel I have anything worthwhile to teach them.
>
> *Belinda (to Geoffrey):* Oh I don't know, they were quite good for me. We began to rehearse a play and they seemed to quite enjoy it.
>
> *Belinda (thinking to herself):* I can see that some of the class can seem quite threatening, but I know I am on top of them and can get through to them. When you get on their wavelength they respond quite well.

Geoffrey is likely to be more defensive than Belinda and therefore tend to blame the class for poor behaviour and a lack of motivation. Because of Belinda's more confident approach (confident both in herself and in the pupils), she is likely to be better able to motivate them to learn and to deal with any difficulties that the class presents without blaming the pupils. Perhaps if each teacher was more open about his or her fears then they could help each other.

Discussion points

a.   Think of a pupil who is highly motivated and think of a pupil who lacks motivation. How might you explain their different levels of motivation in terms of affiliation, agency and autonomy?

b.   How would you rate your own levels of affiliation, agency and autonomy regarding teaching?

What motivates pupils? What the teachers say

Judith: Some children are just happy to learn and are *willing* to learn. They want to do well. We've got some children, they come to school and that's what they expect to do. Other children need more of a push in the right direction. So they need something a bit different. In my class they're often the ones that tend to do more practical, hands on things. When we did the history topic on the Tudors, for many of them the best bit was making clay models of King Henry VIII and his six wives. They really liked that, and most of them can remember the names of all the wives – and especially how they died!

A lot of their motivation comes from marking. I think *your* response to their work motivates them. If *you're* responding to their work, giving them something to work on, so they know where to move themselves forward, I think that motivates them. But you also need to think of something that's not *dull* and not boring. I think it's so hard to sit there, to sit and listen all day is boring. So they want to be *doing* more. That motivates them.

Daniel: I think it's what they've been brought up with, whether they've had *successes*. A child needs to know they're successful. They need to have confidence in themselves, definitely. Also, the lesson needs to be something that they enjoy and is relevant to them. Demotivated children can't see the relevance to them. They don't know *why* they're doing it.

I think demotivation is probably constantly *reinforced*, the same way motivation is probably constantly reinforced, by what's happened to them before. Motivation needs to be something that they've experienced throughout their lives.

Julia: Motivation? Ooh, that's a tricky one. It depends on children's personality, I suppose. We have some children in my class who are just intrinsically motivated by the concept of learning and knowing things and wanting to learn *more*. I think there are other children for whom it's more, 'I've got to pass this target 'cos my mum says so'. It's a tricky one, isn't it? Because I think it's that balancing of the external pressures of *exams* and all those things with actually the *style* of learning that a lot of children have and the two don't necessarily go together. We seem to spend a lot of our time trying to put, you know, square pegs in round holes.

Discussion points

a.   The pupils said that they were motivated to learn by enthusiastic teachers who took them seriously, by lessons that were interesting and challenging, by the physical environment of the classroom and school, by taking part in school clubs and trips, by using ICT and, for some, by the use of rewards. Many pupils said their learning was made harder both by poor behaviour and by how teachers responded to this. In what ways, do you think, the teachers quoted above would agree with these comments?

b.   How do you think these teachers' views relate to the theories of motivation outlined in this chapter – particularly with McLean's 'three As' – affiliation, agency and autonomy?

What motivates pupils? What other researchers say

In 2005, a review of research into secondary pupils' views about motivation was published by the EPPI-Centre, based at the Institute of Education in London (Smith et al. 2005). This report found that pupils are more likely to be motivated to learn if:

* The lessons are perceived as 'fun'.
* The lessons are varied and enable the pupils to actively participate rather than simply listen to someone talking or only reading a text.
* Teachers encourage children to work together in groups.
* Pupils regard the activities as being useful to them and as being linked to the reality of their world outside of school.

The complexity of motivation

Throughout the report, the authors highlighted the complexity of motivation, for example:

> The relationship between particular sets of beliefs and motivational behaviours is not a simple one; pupil beliefs are more likely to be part of a complex set of factors that will combine to create a particular motivational profile.
>
> (Smith et al. 2005, p. 56)

By this they mean that pupils will have different motivational responses to different aspects of school life – they might be motivated to learn English but not maths, or to engage in science but not with history. They present a 'profile' rather than a simple 'picture' of motivation. This ties in with the 'webs of significance' discussed on p. 24. Each pupil will have their own unique 'web' of aspects of school life, out-of-school activity and interests and home situation which will shape their experience of motivation.

There is no simple 'cause and effect' when it comes to pupil motivation; a range of factors are always involved, such as external circumstances, the personalities and characters of the individual pupils and family background. The motivational stance adopted by any one pupil is going to be a result of the interaction of all of these (and more) factors. 'Motivation for learning is a complex overarching concept, which is influenced by a range of psychosocial factors both internal to the learner and present in the learner's social and natural environment' (Harlen and Deakin-Crick 2003, p. 173).

A final word

Given all the complexity of the classroom and the people within it, Radford (2006, pp. 184–185) states that the teacher is not so much a 'bulldozer' pushing through an academic 'vision', but:

> is more in the position of the canoeist shooting the rapids continuously adapting in the face of unknown and unpredictable challenges and with sufficient information only to respond to the local and the immediate.

Discussion points

a.   Why is a teacher or teaching assistant not a 'bulldozer'?
b.   Why is it more appropriate to see a teacher or a teaching assistant as a canoeist shooting the rapids?
c.   Central to this chapter is engaging the pupil voice that is asking them what they see as motivating. This can be done, as in research by Hutchins (2010), not by giving children a questionnaire to fill out, nor sitting them down and asking them a range of predetermined structured questions, but rather providing them with an opportunity to discuss together what is important to them. Letting pupils have their say could also be achieved by asking pupils considered and searching questions. What considered and searching questions could you ask?

Summary

In this chapter we have looked at:

What pupils have said about what helps and what hinders their learning. We have discovered that pupils' motivation to learn is greatly impacted by how teachers:

- structure lessons
- vary lesson content and teaching style
- relate to pupils, and
- deal with challenging behaviour.

How pupils see themselves as learners. We have seen that the extent to which pupils see themselves as being successful learners in school is affected:

- by the way teachers treat them
- by the physical environment in which they are expected to learn, and
- by a range of emotional and psychological factors.

How a number of educational researchers and practitioners have approached theories of motivation. Although each one has a distinct approach, there is also a good deal of overlap, both with each other and with what the pupils said:

- the role of the teacher is crucial
- the relationship between extrinsic motivation (receiving rewards for learning) and intrinsic motivation (engaging in learning for its own sake) is not straightforward
- pupils need to feel a sense of belonging in the school and classroom which means they identify with the values and aims of the school
- pupils need to feel they have some measure of control over both what is being taught and the way they are expected to learn
- pupils need to feel that what they are being asked to learn is within their reach, but is sufficiently challenging to make their effort worthwhile.

What teachers have said about pupil motivation. The level of motivation experienced by pupils is shaped:

- by factors within the child, such as personality or the level of confidence he or she has in themselves to learn
- by marking – what teachers write in their books
- by pupils' past experiences of learning
- by the perceived relevance of the subject matter
- by the tension between a fixed curriculum and pupils' own learning styles.

Chapter 5

Motivating students through assessment

An overview

This chapter begins with a story.

The way I see it: Judith's story

> You're constantly assessing the children – not necessarily on paper, but just watching them, seeing how they're taking in what you are teaching, how they respond. I think it's really important, a massive part of the role. I think assessment is *me* watching and taking in what I'm seeing about the children. I question and observe them, get things from the children and see where they are. If I think the majority of my children have achieved what my aim was at the beginning of the lesson, that's OK. Obviously, if they haven't then we have to go back and revisit things.

For Judith, assessment is a key part of her role as a teacher, and assessment plays a key part in motivating pupils. Another teacher committed to motivating pupils through assessment, Diane, uses the term 'evaluation sandwich' with her classes. By this she means she gives one positive/good point (the first slice of the sandwich), one point for growth or improvement (the middle section of the sandwich), followed by another good point (the other slice of the sandwich). As a matter of principle she applies the 'evaluation sandwich' to all her lessons – through both her verbal feedback and her marking of pupils' work. By this strategy she ensures she gives twice the amount of positive comments to negative. Diane is aware that the process by which she assesses their work plays a significant role in how motivated pupils are to learn. More negative than positive responses would, in her view, damage pupils' self-esteem and lower their motivation to learn.

But the link between assessment and motivation is not clear cut. For one thing, 'assessment', like everything else in education, is not as straightforward as it may seem.

The term 'assessment' derives from the Latin word *assidere*, meaning 'to sit beside'. Considered like this, it sounds almost cosy, but there is an edge to it. One aim, for sure, is to sit beside someone in order to come to understand them, but a second aim is to weigh up that person's strengths and weaknesses. Biddy Youell (2006, p. 147) argues that 'all forms of testing or appraisal carry with them the possibility of success or the fear of failure'. As Bethan Marshall and Dylan Wiliam state, 'Assessment . . . is, after all, a type of judgement' (2006, p. 4). Teachers and teaching assistants should always be mindful of this facet of assessment when they talk with pupils or mark their work. Assessment of any kind can enhance pupils' confidence in themselves and in their ability to learn – but it can also have the exact opposite effect. Both *what* is done and *how* it is done, in terms of assessment in the classroom, is crucial.

Types of assessment

Within schools, pupils are likely to encounter four types of assessment – two certainly and two possibly, depending on their level of learning needs. The two most common forms of assessment are *summative* and *formative*. The two less common forms are *diagnostic* and *dynamic* assessments.

Summative assessment

Summative assessment is, as its name suggests, a summation of what pupils have learnt. It usually takes the form of more formal testing at the end of a topic or unit of work. The most obvious summative assessments experienced by pupils in schools in England are the Standard Attainment Tests (SATs) given at the end of Key Stage 2 and the GCSEs at the end of Key Stage 4. These forms of assessment measure pupils against national standards, rather than against their own past performance. Any form of test or exam at the end of a unit of work or a period of teaching (such as end of year tests) is summative; however, the results can be used in a formative way.

> ### Case study 5.1: Summative assessment can be used in a formative way
>
> At the end of May, Daniel's year 4 class sit a maths test using a paper produced by the QCA (Qualification and Curriculum Authority). As a result of a combination of the results of this test and Daniel's teacher assessment, each pupil is given a national curriculum level in maths. This goes on their report home to parents and is also placed on the school's electronic database of results. The levels the pupils achieve in this way are used to place them in maths sets for the next academic year and their papers are discussed at length between various teachers to see where each pupil's strengths and weaknesses lie. Plans are put in place to respond to these findings. In this way, although the tests are summative, in that they examine what the children have learnt during year 4, they are used formatively to help plan and structure teaching for the year ahead.

The implications of summative assessment are many and varied, and are often argued over. There is a danger to how children might view themselves in the light of the results of these sorts of assessment: 'I'm a level 5 in maths but only a level 3 in English.' Too much emphasis may be placed on these 'end results', especially if measures of pupil progress are only made via such summative assessments. How a child performs in a single test on a particular day might be very different to how they would perform on another day. Another potential danger to which summative assessments could lead is the possibility of children (and teachers) viewing themselves as 'failures' or 'successes'. For a child who consistently gets low marks in tests, this could lead to a self-fulfilling prophecy: 'I am not good at tests, I cannot learn, therefore I won't even try.' Pupils who consistently see themselves as 'failing' in summative assessments are likely to be demotivated and switched off learning. Pupils who consistently do well in tests might be motivated to work harder and learn more but, if they measure their success only in terms of test results, they may actually be demotivated to attempt challenging learning tasks, choosing instead to stay within their learning 'comfort zones' so as to ensure continued exam success (for further discussion, see pp. 58–59).

Formative assessment

Formative assessment is more of an ongoing process of finding out how well pupils are learning what is being taught whilst it is still in the process of being taught. This type of assessment is able to inform teachers' planning for future lessons. It also provides the opportunity for pupils themselves to see how they are doing and to agree targets for their next steps in learning. Much of formative assessment is likely to be informal although, as we have seen, more formal tests can be used in a formative way. Formative assessment can be used to measure a pupil's progress against his or her own past performance. It does not in itself measure pupils either against national standards or against each other. In this way, the stigma of 'failure' or the false suggestion of 'success' can be avoided. Used effectively, formative assessment can promote pupil motivation because students are able to see how much progress they have made, what they are doing well and are given feedback as to how they can improve. They are not left in the dark by positive but over-general teacher comments such as 'good work' or 'well done' (what was 'good' about it or in what way did they 'do well'?), nor by negative but equally general comments such as 'could do better' or 'try to improve' (in what way could I 'do better' or how can I 'improve'?).

To put it succinctly, if over-simply, summative assessment is assessment *of* learning, whereas formative assessment is assessment *for* learning.

Diagnostic assessment

Ordinary formative and summative assessment will give information about the pupils' current learning levels and needs, but for some pupils more detailed diagnostic assessments will need to take place. These will normally be carried out on an individual basis, conducted by either the school's Special Educational Needs Co-ordinator (SENCo) or external professionals such as educational psychologists. Diagnostic assessments attempt to identify specific areas of difficulty experienced by the pupil, such as limited working memory (how much information a person can hold in his mind at any one point in time and use to perform tasks), left–right orientation confusion (distinguishing, for example, between letters or symbols facing left and facing right – the classic 'b–d reversal') or difficulty with phonological awareness (for instance, whether a pupil can detect rhyme). An example of diagnostic assessment would be a reading test which not only gives a reading accuracy and comprehension age, but also an indication of the areas of difficulty in reading or understanding experienced by a pupil. Other examples would include screening tests for dyslexia (difficulty with reading and/or spelling) or dyscalculia (difficulty with numbers).

Dynamic assessment

Based on the educational learning theories of the Russian educationalist Lev Vygotsky (1978, 1986), dynamic assessments seek to inquire not so much into the current levels of a pupil's learning as into their capacity for future learning. Vygotsky emphasised the social context of children's learning. Learning does not happen in isolation from others. A more experienced learner – a parent or teacher – is needed to lead a child to further learning. Parents, teachers and teaching assistants support children in their development of knowledge. They prompt them, offer suggestions and give corrections, but as the child grows older and learns more, that level and type of support is no longer needed. Or, at least, it is not needed for the same things: as the saying goes, 'what children can do with help today, they will be able to do by themselves tomorrow'.

However, children differ in the extent to which they are able to learn or in the pace of that learning. This is what Vygotsky means by the term 'the zone of proximal development' (ZPD). Two children may score the same in a test on the same day but, after instruction, if tested again, one may make more progress than the other. The one who has made more progress has a greater learning capacity or ZPD than the other. This has implications for our understanding of children's potential – the child with the greater ZPD has a greater potential for learning than a child with a lesser ZPD. Dynamic assessments can be both formal and informal, but always seek to find out something about a pupil's ZPD.

Principles relating to assessment

Whatever form the assessment takes, three principles apply to it – the principles of *validity, reliability* and *engagement*.

Validity

To be valid, an assessment must actually assess what it sets out to assess. If the assessment is a maths assessment, it must test the pupil's mathematical knowledge and not some other kind of knowledge. So, for example, a pupil sitting a maths test may need someone to read the questions for him if he has difficulty reading, otherwise the test is a test of his reading ability and will not necessarily measure his maths knowledge at all. Similarly, for a pupil new to the English language, a translation of the test into her first language may be necessary in order to validly assess her knowledge of a subject.

Reliability

Put simply, reliability means that if another person assessed the pupil, the result would be the same, or at least similar. The issue here is whether the person giving the assessment influences the pupil in such a way as to affect the result. A teacher in one class marking a piece of written work and discussing areas for improvement with the pupils should be making suggestions similar to another teacher in a parallel class. This is where the concept of 'moderation' comes in, whereby teachers work together to ensure consistency within a school and, indeed, across schools.

Engagement with the assessment

Sally and Charles sit the same test. They score the same marks. Does this mean they are at the same ability level? Does this mean they have the same level of motivation?

It depends – if they put the same amount of effort in, then the answer is probably 'yes'. However, Sally worked hard at the test – she engaged with the assessment. Charles, on the other hand, did not. He did not prepare for it. He did not take it seriously. He wrote down a few random thoughts rather than giving a considered argument.

What does this show? It shows that Sally's score or level is likely to be a more 'accurate' indicator of where she is in her learning than Charles's score.

A basis of all assessment is that pupils are engaging with that assessment or piece of work to the best of their ability. This is especially so when that assessment is designed to give them a score, mark or level of some kind. Similarly, in a diagnostic screening test for dyslexia, two pupils may come out as being 'at risk' of being dyslexic but, if one pupil did not engage with the test at all, his 'identification' is suspect.

So – there are all sorts of things to bear in mind when considering any form of assessment – both in the giving of assessments and in the use made of the results of assessments. Nevertheless, assessment is necessary and is an essential part of school life. Knowing where pupils are in their learning is necessary if teaching is to be effective. Learning can only take place where the teaching connects with the pupils in a way they can understand and to which they can relate, and where teaching moves the pupils on in some way, i.e. it cannot be too far ahead of them so that they do not understand what is being taught, but neither can it be something which they know already. This relates to setting suitably challenging work which motivates pupils to want to learn (see pp. 32, 36, 51). In order to pitch the curriculum at an appropriate level, teachers need to assess their pupils. Assessment can either be formal, such as via tests, or informal, such as through teacher observation.

In this chapter, the focus is on formative assessment. One reason for this is that much is made in government documentation and in educational research of the role that formative assessment/assessment for learning can have in promoting the motivation of pupils, and it is to this we now turn.

What *is* Assessment for Learning?

Case study 5.2: Mrs Crowther's lesson

At the start of a literacy lesson in year 6, Mrs Crowther has displayed the following on the interactive whiteboard:

Learning objective: To be able to use time-connectives to sequence events
Remember:
    Chronological order
    Refer to time connectives from previous lesson/flipchart
    Full punctuation
On the flip chart, is a list of time connectives:
    First
    Afterwards
    Following that
    Since then
    Meanwhile
    Lastly
    Subsequently

Mrs Crowther gives instructions to the class. They need to write what has happened to them so far that day in sequence. She projects onto the whiteboard a piece of text she has prepared concerning *her* day and reads it to the class. The children discuss it. She then asks two questions, 'What are the time connectives I have used?' and 'What do the time connectives do?' After the class has discussed this, she asks the children to begin writing in their books.

Within this period of ten minutes, Mrs Crowther has used three of the 'Assessment for Learning' (AfL) strategies:

1. First, she has given the class the **aim of the lesson** – to be able to use time connectives to sequence events. Through discussion with the class she has made sure that they all understand what 'time connectives' means. She has written some examples of time connectives on a flipchart in the room.
2. Second, she has given the class **success criteria** (which in this school are called 'Remember To' points). These are what the children need to do in order to achieve the aim of the lesson.
3. Third, she has presented the class with a **model** or example of what a good piece of work looks like – she has written it herself using all of the Remember To points. She gives the class the opportunity to discuss why this piece of work achieves the aims of the lesson.

So – what *is* assessment for learning and why is it important to look at it?

The importance of AfL

Considerable claims are made for AfL, for example:

*   AfL improves learning – standards are raised (Black and Wiliam 1998, p. 61).
*   AfL stimulates motivation and self-esteem (Harlen and Deakin-Crick 2002, p. 10).

The nature of AfL

A group of educationalists called the Assessment Reform Group (ARG) summarised the principles of AfL:

Assessment for Learning is the process of seeking and interpreting evidence for use by learners and their teachers to decide where the learners are in their learning, where they need to go and how best to get there.

(Assessment Reform Group 2002)

For AfL to be effective, the following strategies must be applied consistently in the classroom:

*   Learning goals (for the pupils) and learning objectives/intentions (of the lesson) are shared so that pupils understand what they are aiming for.
*   Feedback from the teacher should relate to the learning objectives and help pupils identify how they can improve.

- Time must be given for pupils to respond to this feedback.
- Teachers and pupils must be involved in reflecting on the learning taking place.
- Pupils need to be taught self-assessment techniques enabling them to become responsible for their own learning.
- Peer-assessment needs to be encouraged and planned for in a 'safe' learning environment.

This sounds simple and, taken at a simplistic level, it is: you as the teacher or the teaching assistant follow the above principles and procedures and your pupils will be motivated to learn and will improve. However, the situation is altogether more complex.

In an attempt to work through this complexity, a number of educationalists have introduced concepts which will be helpful in our consideration of motivation through assessment.

The spirit and the letter of AfL

Marshall and Drummond (2006, p. 136) introduce the distinction between the 'spirit' and the 'letter' of AfL. Teachers who have grasped the 'technique' of AfL but have not understood the principles behind it, or teachers who seek to implement AfL 'strategies' only because they have been told to by their school leadership team, may be in danger of simply keeping to the 'letter' of AfL: 'I've given a learning objective, I've put up some success criteria, I tell the pupils what they need to do to improve – there, I've done assessment for learning.'

Alternatively, Julia, a junior school teacher, gives some insight into what engaging with the 'spirit' of AfL may be like:

> It's tricky isn't it? I think most of the strategies and ideas that come into school I think have a lot of *value*, but I don't always like having to apply them to every lesson. It reminds me a little too much sometimes of the 'This is what I'm going to teach you – there, I've taught it to you, you know, show the green card if you've learned it – let's move on.' And I think to some extent that sometimes fits in with a very much box-ticking mentality. [This would be in keeping with the 'letter' of AfL.]

> I think you have to have a certain degree of flexibility or confidence to use AfL as a tool rather than simply follow it as a technique. [Using AfL as a *tool* is the essence of the 'spirit' of AfL.] Some lessons fit AfL really well, others do not. I think it's the idea of AfL being a *tool* that's important. There are some times when you want to use it, and that I think is down to your professional judgement. So, for instance, when I teach adding hundreds, tens and units using the column method I can have a clear learning objective: to learn to add hundreds, tens and units using the column method. There are also definite success criteria such as 'numbers are written out in the correct columns', 'numbers are placed under each other in each of the columns' and 'numbers are carried into the next column if needed.' But I think if it is 'in our school we're going to do lessons *this* way, and that's what we want to see in 90 per cent of our lessons', then you run the risk of it just becoming a list of ticks, and the children *tick* things and they're not doing the thinking behind it. You're spoon-feeding them assessment. [Again referring to the 'letter' of AfL.]

AFL is only part of what happens in class

No aspect of learning and education takes place in isolation – everything needs to fit together. Assessment does not take place separately to teaching, behaviour management, the physical environment of the classroom, and so on. The bottom line is – *all* education involves social interaction. As teachers interact with teaching assistants and they both interact with pupils, and as pupils interact with each other and with the adults in their class, so a classroom 'environment' is established. And within this environment, assessment takes place. Assessment, too, is an example of social interaction: 'Educational assessment must be understood as a *social* practice, an art as much as a science' (Broadfoot and Black 2004, p. 8).

Whether or not AfL strategies really do improve pupil motivation or not depends to a large extent on what sort of classroom environment has been created.

Case study 5.3: The classroom environment

Someone has set the school fire alarm off. The whole school has been disrupted and the teachers need to find out who did it. Each of them is asked by the head teacher to talk with his or her class about it. Two teachers go about this in very different ways.

Mr Kneasden shouts at his class: 'I'm certain that one of you lot did it. Now – own up or else!'

Miss Mapleton speaks very calmly to her class: 'It was a silly thing that happened, but it might have been an accident. If any of you know anything about it please come and talk to me privately and we can take it further.'

How does this have anything to do with assessment for learning?

The answer is this – the spirit of AfL necessitates nurturing a positive classroom learning environment. If the responses of these two teachers to that particular situation are typical of the way they conduct themselves in class and the way they develop their relationships with the pupils, then the pupils in Miss Mapleton's class are likely to be far more responsive to her AfL strategies than they are in Mr Kneasden's class. They are likely to trust her, respect her and listen to her. Pupils in Mr Kneasden's class may well resent him deeply. They have each created a 'classroom environment', but one is a lot more positive and constructive than the other. Both teachers may 'use' AfL and follow similar procedures, but one will be exercising the 'spirit' of AfL while the other merely the 'letter' of AfL. It is not hard to tell which is which.

Assessment as Learning

There is a danger that providing too much formative assessment structure, such as learning objectives and success criteria, can make pupils *more* rather than *less* dependent upon teachers, thereby defeating the object of giving pupils the knowledge and skills to be independent learners. This problem is termed 'assessment *as* learning' by Torrance (2007, p. 281): where 'criteria compliance' replaces learning.

What is meant by 'criteria compliance'?

Take the case study of Mrs Crowther's literacy lesson. Some of the children might write a paragraph, look at it and think:
   'Right, have I followed the Remember To points?

1. I've written in chronological order – what I did first, then second, then third – yes, tick that one.
2. I've used some of the time connectives Miss put on the flipchart – at first, then, next – yes, tick that one.
3. And I've put full stops, capital letters and commas in – yes, tick that one.

   There, I've finished my work and it's good.'
   The message being conveyed is that learning is equal to ticking boxes – the more boxes ticked, the more learning has occurred. This may to some extent be true, but such learning is likely to be surface learning rather than deep learning (see Chapter 1).
   This sort of thing is an example of 'criteria compliance' whereby assessment actually becomes the learning rather than a means to establishing the depth of learning that has taken place. In this situation, learning is seen purely as meeting the demands of the assessment. It is doubtful that these children actually did write 'good' pieces of work: it would more likely be that their writing was very stilted. 'Deep learning' (pp. 14–15) requires more of the children than this.

Case study 5.4: A learning task

A class of year 5 pupils are writing a recount of the story of Sweeney Todd, the demon barber of Fleet Street, as part of their Victorians topic. They have been given success criteria of: write in the first person; write in chronological order using time connective sentence openers; include adjectives for descriptive detail; write a personal response.
   Mary wrote the following:

One dark and gloomy evening I was walking down narrow, crowded Fleet Street. Out of the corner of my eye I spotted the weird, spooky, ghostly barber's shop. There was a greenish-blue light inside so I looked in. Then I saw a strange bearded man in the chair with the fat, ugly, crazed barber giving him a shave. Following that, I noticed this evil man put his wrinkled hand on a golden lever at the side of the black leather chair which was covered in red spots. Suddenly, the bearded man, who had a glint of fear in his eyes, screamed – the barber had slit his throat with the razor-sharp razor. After that the barber laughed crazily and pulled hard on the golden lever and the man, whose rich clothes were now covered in blood, disappeared into a large, gaping hole into the pitch blackness of a sickening cellar. I ran away terrified feeling sick to the depths of my aching stomach.

The teacher asked the class to assess their own pieces of work before handing them in to be marked by him. He asked the pupils to highlight in their work where they had met the success criteria. Mary highlighted a lot of her work and felt very pleased with it – she had met all of the success criteria. She had written in the first person (tick the box), she had written in chronological order using time connectives at the openings of her sentences (tick the box), she had included adjectives to give detailed descriptions (tick the box), and she had written a personal response (all the boxes ticked).

Discussion points

a.   Is what Mary wrote a *good* piece of writing or has she merely used the success criteria in a mechanical way, like some kind of checklist? Essentially, is her use of adjectives and time connectives *appropriate*?

b.   Should her work be considered as 'criteria compliant' or an effective piece of writing?

Summary

Assessment for Learning, then, is not so much a technique as a way of teaching. It comes out of a way of looking at learning and at pupils that encourages social interaction. People engaging with it must believe that *all* children can make progress and that they can be helped in this process by adults and by each other.

Teachers

What teachers say about AfL

Here, some teachers talk about their approach to Assessment for Learning. Mertler (2009) writes about the 'assessment literacy' of teachers – how much or how little they really understand about assessment and, in particular, formative assessment (AfL). As you read these comments made by teachers, consider what level of 'assessment literacy' you think that they show.

DANIEL

Daniel, reflecting on the spirit of AfL, talks about how AfL underpins the whole of his teaching. It is not a 'bolt-on' addition for him:

> I think, for me as a teacher, AfL is a way of understanding what's happening in the lesson: understanding whether they're getting the concept, whether I need to move on, whether I need to slow down, whether I need to revisit it, where the misconceptions are. It's kind of a guide, testing the waters almost. If I was on a boat, it would be like reading my instruments to see if I were on course. It's those little 'stop-checks' to see where you're going. I think, for the children, it's time to stop and to evaluate and to think, 'Where am I going with this? Do I understand it?' It gives them the chance to think about the purpose of what they're doing. It also helps them see the next step. They can see the process of learning better.

JULIA

Julia, again reflecting on the spirit of AfL, focuses on how children in her class take part in the AfL process:

> My understanding of it is involving children in the process of assessing their learning so that they know what they need to do next. We would do that either through responding to marking or just questioning them and having a conversation with them about what they've done and what they're doing at the time. I like the principle of it 'cos I think it's exactly that idea of getting them involved and thinking about what they need to do next.

REBEKAH

Rebekah, speaking about her personal engagement with AfL, talks about enjoyment and awareness raising, both for herself as a teacher and for the children – another aspect of the spirit of AfL. But she is also realistic about the difficulties of putting AfL into practice:

> AfL should be on the spot, a daily basis. It's an awareness of learning the whole time. [Speaking about the years 1999–2001 when she first heard about AfL.] AfL was very new and it was one of my favourite times in teaching. I thought it was absolutely wonderful and it changed my perception of a lesson – making the children so much more aware and more involved in their step-by-step learning. I think it just changed my idea of 'Why are you doing something?', 'How are they going to learn from it?' and 'How are you going to explain to them how they are learning from it and what is their response going to be?'

> At the beginning, everything seemed straightforward, easy – this is the solution, this is going to make things better. And then, so many years down the line, it all seems much harder again. It's not a0s straightforward as 'Here you are children, you do this, you respond to it, you understand it, you'll get better.' That doesn't happen in a straightforward way. You know, learning is a very complex.

For all three of these teachers, AfL is not so much a strategy as a process – a process of engaging with the children and engaging the children in their learning. And for all three, an essential aspect of this is holding conversations with pupils about their work, as opposed to simply telling them what to do and what to correct. Teaching assistants can participate in this as much as teachers, as the following case study shows.

Case study 5.5: Pupil conferencing

Let's go back to Mary, who wrote that recount of Sweeney Todd. Her teacher took her book in, read what she had written, including her self-assessment, and realised that, although she had technically achieved the aim, there was a lot to discuss about the passage. Rather than mark it in writing, he asked the teaching assistant in her class, Miss Smith, to hold an individual pupil conference with Mary. Here is part of that conversation:

Miss Smith: Mary, I can see you have worked really hard on this story. How do you feel about it?

Mary: I really enjoyed writing it. The story is so horrible, it's wonderful.

Miss Smith: I can tell you enjoyed doing it – your enthusiasm comes through it all. And you have used the Remember To points to help you write it. I'd like us to look together, though, at how you have used adjectives in the text.

Mary: Yes, I thought you might. I wasn't sure at the time, but I wanted to include lots of detail like Sir told us to.

Miss Smith: I can see that, but let's read one of your sentences together. How about the first one? You wrote: *One dark and gloomy evening I was walking down narrow, crowded Fleet Street.* How many adjectives have you put in there do you think?

Mary: Um, I'd say four.

Miss Smith: I'd agree – do you think you need them all? Does it help the sentence to have so many?

Mary: Probably not. But I like the opening part – I think that saying the evening was 'dark and gloomy' helps say what it was like. It's kind of spooky, and I like that.

Miss Smith: I like that too – it's what we call 'atmospheric'. So let's keep that in. But what do you think about describing Fleet Street as being 'narrow and crowded'?

Mary: I don't know really. Not sure.

Miss Smith: Do you think it adds anything to the story at this point? Personally, I think you might have too many adjectives in this sentence. The street might have been narrow, but I'm not sure you need to say it here. But what about the 'crowded' bit? Let's think about that a little. If it was crowded, do you think you would be the only one looking through the barber's window?

Mary: No, I suppose not. Lots of people would have seen what was going on. It would have been better to say the street was empty.

Miss Smith: So there are two things for you to think about: how *many* adjectives you use and what *sort* of adjectives you use. You were right – using description was one of our Remember To points, but it's important to think whether the descriptions you are using are appropriate or necessary. Now let's look at the rest of the recount.

By holding a conversation, Miss Smith was able to discuss matters with Mary in far greater detail than the teacher could ever have written in his marking of her work. The conversation also meant that Mary could express her views as well. Pupil conferencing like this can take a bit of time, but it is worth it.

What influences teachers' approaches to AfL?

A number of underlying factors crucially affect a teacher's approach to formative assessment:

- The more teachers understand the principles and the practice of AfL, the more effective they are likely to be in its implementation.
- Their beliefs about the nature of learning are going to have an impact on their assessment practice. Those who see learning as taking place when teachers and pupils relate to each other, rather than the teacher simply talking at the children, are more likely to view AfL positively.
- A teacher's perception of pupils and their ability, or lack of it, to make progress and succeed in school will also have a major impact on their approach to formative

assessment. For AfL to be 'successful', teachers must believe that all pupils have the ability to make progress and benefit from the strategies of formative assessment.

- Teachers require a range of skills and knowledge to engage with formative assessment, such as being able to understand what might cause errors in pupils' work, being able to provide a model of what good learning might look like, and being able to understand how learning is understood by their pupils.
- They must be able to frame 'feedback statements' in 'language that is already known and understood by the learners' (Sadler 1998, p. 82).
- To regulate learning, teachers must be able to put themselves in the position of the learner who is struggling.
- They must be skilled in planning for formative assessment (Webb and Jones 2009). Formative assessment does not happen by accident.

Discussion points

a.   How do the views expressed by teachers (on pp. 115–116) relate to the list of factors given above?

b.   To what extent do you think their views would help motivate pupils to learn?

c.   Which aspects might hinder motivation, or what else would you have expected them to comment upon in order to promote learner motivation?

Pupils

No learning takes place without the learner.

(Perrenoud 1998, p. 86)

Case study 5.6: Pupils' responses to feedback

Mrs Crowther has marked the pupils' books, in which each has written in sequence about his or her day using time connectives. Two pupils, Julian and Sasha, have received similar feedback comments:

'Well done, this is well written. You have used interesting time connectives. Next time check on your punctuation before you hand in a piece of work.'

Julian thinks, 'Oh good. Miss really liked my work. I must remember to put in punctuation properly next time I write.'

Sasha thinks, 'Oh no, not again. Miss is always picking on me. Why does she always have to have a go at me about my punctuation? She doesn't really mean it when she says she liked my work, besides, I didn't have anything to write about. My life is so boring.'

Whenever work is being handed back, Julian looks forward to it and is eager to see what his teacher has written, knowing that her comments are helping him to learn. The opposite is true of Sasha. She dreads the time at which books are handed back. She is convinced the teacher will say something nasty about her and her work. She thinks she is 'rubbish' at her work, and that nothing the teacher can do or say can help her.

How pupils respond and participate in AfL will be a major factor in how effective AfL is. For Julian, AfL is likely to be effective, but not for Sasha. Why is this?

Various aspects of pupils' lives are identified as influencing their engagement with, and response to, formative assessment:

- Their motivation and self-perception – how they see themselves as people and as learners in school (Black and Wiliam 1998; Brookhart 2001). Some pupils are motivated to succeed, whilst others are motivated to avoid failure (see p. 32).
- Their beliefs about their capacity to learn (Black and Wiliam 1998) – self-efficacy (see pp. 34, 53).
- The sort of assessment and 'teacher disposition' experienced in previous classes (Sadler 1998; Brookhart 2001; Moni et al. 2002). In the case study of the school fire alarm being set off (p. 113), Mr Kneasden's 'disposition' is very different from that of Miss Mapleton. A pupil who has experienced a year of Mr Kneasden may take quite a long time to respond positively in the more conducive learning environment of Miss Mapleton's class.
- Their emotional response to assessment (Moni et al. 2002) – for example, whether they perceive the task as being worthwhile.
- The 'myriad of other cultural contexts' which they experience outside school and which impact on their learning (Elwood 2006, p. 228) – what pupils do and experience when they are not in school will have an enormous influence on how they respond when they are in school.
- Their ability and/or willingness to identify with the learning culture of the classroom – to see themselves as 'belonging' or 'not belonging' (Black and Wiliam 1998; Brookhart 2001; Moni et al. 2002). This links with communities of practice (see pp. 15–16).
- Pupil agency – to what extent they see themselves as having control over their learning or whether they see learning as something that simply 'happens' to them (Black and Wiliam 2006, linking with McLean's 'three As' (p. 99).

As Black and Wiliam (1998, p. 21) state, pupils are not 'passive recipients of a call to action'; rather there are complex links between the message given, the way it is received, and the motivation which ensures action is taken.

For Julian, all of the above are likely to be positive – he wants to learn, he sees himself as a good learner, he believes he has the ability to learn more, his previous experiences of teachers are likely to have been a happy and his emotional response to the teacher's marking is one of anticipation and joy. Quite probably his life outside of school reinforces what he is experiencing inside school, he identifies with the classroom, feeling he belongs and he feels he has some control over his learning – he can make it better for himself.

Sasha, on the other hand, is the complete opposite. She might want to learn, but feels she can't – she sees herself as a 'poor' learner, someone who finds learning difficult. She does not think she is capable of making much progress in her learning, no matter how much effort she puts in and whatever the teacher says about her. In previous classes, she feels that teachers did not like her and viewed her as being badly behaved. She dreads receiving teacher feedback and is ashamed of her work. Outside school, her home situation and what she gets up to in her spare time has no place for academic work. She sees the classroom as being very different to her life and does not feel she belongs. Finally, she does not feel that she has any control over her learning – learning is something that happens *to* her and is put upon her by teachers.

Discussion points

a. Why do you think these two children responded in such different ways?
b. What could be done, do you think, to change the way Sasha views herself?
c. What, if any, dangers do you see in how Julian approaches his work?

Learning goals/learning objectives

For AfL to be effective in both motivating pupils and moving their learning forward, one key aspect needs to be clarity over the learning intentions of a lesson. Dylan Wiliam sees this as the first strategy that needs to be put into place because 'before one can begin to design effective activities for learners, one has to be clear about what one wants the students to be able to do' (Wiliam 2009, pp. 11–12). The teacher needs to be clear, but this clarity needs to be communicated to the learners in ways which they both understand and to which they can relate and engage. They need to understand where the lesson is going (the learning intention) and be able to recognise when they have got there (criteria for success).

Teachers, however, are not always 'clear' about the aim of their lessons. It can take some deliberation over what the learning objective (what they want the children to actually *learn* in the lesson) is to be, as this junior school teacher points out:

> I think teachers understand the *importance* of learning objectives, but I must admit when we're sat down planning as a year group, the learning objective could take us ten minutes to sit and think about because it's not straightforward. You're trying to sum up the *learning* in a lesson, like the key. You're trying to distil the key aspect of that lesson in a sentence and, for some lessons, you might be doing a couple of activities, but you're trying to think, 'Right, what is the specific *learning*?' So it *is* difficult and I don't always get it right.
>
> The other week, for instance, the three of us year group teachers were planning our literacy lessons for the next week. We were doing a unit on poetry. At first we thought the learning objective should be something like, 'To be able to write a poem.' But we realised this was too general. We spent a long time just talking about what a poem was, and in the end we gave up. Instead, we decided to focus on one particular aspect of poetry in each lesson, like, 'To use metaphor to describe an event or a person.'

A key question in AfL is whether pupils have a clear idea of what learning objectives are and what they are for. In the discussion below, the two pupils talking show their understanding of learning objectives, and from where the teachers get the learning objectives.

Case study 5.7: Where do learning objectives come from?

Dawn: Learning objectives are targets. You have to achieve them, like do them. We obey them.
Linda: The aim tells you what to do. We get them from the teacher.
Dawn: And the teacher gets them from their imagination.

Linda: No, the head teacher sets them work for the children.

Dawn: The head teacher gets them, and head teacher gets them from God, the head teacher of all time!

Discussion points

a. How do these pupils see a learning goal? Is it an *aide memoire*, a command or something else?
b. What is the connection between how they see a learning goal and their perceptions of learning?
c. What is the connection between pupils' views about learning goals and their motivations to engage with that learning? For instance, does viewing learning goals as commands encourage deep or surface learning (see pp. 14–15)?

Success criteria

Pupils need to know when they have achieved the learning aim. This is what effective criteria for success provide – a measure against which pupils can assess their own work to see to what extent they have met the aim of the lesson. For success criteria to work, three aspects are needed: they need to be understood by pupils, they need to relate to pupils' learning experiences and they need to be used by pupils in the way in which they were designed to be used.

What the pupils say: How do they see success criteria or 'Remember To' points?

Dawn: You have to check through the Remember To points and see what you've done. If you haven't done the Remember To points, then you haven't done it right.

Simon: From *my* point of view, Remember To is like a plan to learn what to do for my work. Sometimes I *do* use it as a plan. If the work's a bit hard, I can read it and see what to do.

Philip: The thing I like about Remember To points is that you can look back at that and if you done something wrong you could just look at the Remember To points and then go, 'Oh yeah' and notice that it's wrong and then change it. They kind of give you help without someone talking to us, because it tells you kind of what to do.

Matthew: And we had the sheet of Remember To points and once we'd done that in the story, in chronological order, we'd tick it off so we knew what we'd done when we done it.

These pupils are very positive about their use of Remember To points, in that they are using them to guide their work, but, nevertheless, their comments raise questions. Are their views likely to lead to deep learning or to surface learning (criteria compliance)? Should they be developing their own list of Remember To points (i.e. exercising self-regulation – see pp. 61–62)?

What the pupils say: What's wrong with Remember To points?

Esther: I don't really look at the Remember To points, to be honest. She always says the same thing.

Benjamin: I don't like it when they say put in capital letters and full stops.

Sarah: Yeah, 'cos that's like, baby learning.

Thomas: They don't really help. They never tell you what you need to know.

Ruth: She sort of says, 'Remember full stops, use good description.' And in literacy and stuff like that, it's like, 'Yeah, but we were going to do that anyway.' I've kind of stopped looking now.

Discussion points

a. What, in your view, caused these pupils to respond positively to success criteria?
b. What led them to respond negatively?
c. What implications for learning and motivation could you draw from these observations?

Feedback

Feedback is one of the most important aspects of AfL, but both *what* is being fed back to pupils and *when* it is being fed back is crucial to the effectiveness of its use.

Content of feedback

With regards to the *what*, 'Well done, that was good' or 'You really need to improve' are both types of feedback (of sorts), but neither is constructive. The former begs the questions, 'What was good about it? In what ways was it good? How can I tell in future what is going to be good as well?' The latter comment tells the pupil absolutely nothing. Constructive feedback, either verbally or in written form via marking, needs to state what has been achieved by the pupil and/or what needs to be done to improve. Being specific and detailed is the key. Constructive feedback needs to relate to the learning objectives of the lesson and the learning goals of the pupils. Teachers and teaching assistants need to phrase their comments in such a way that the pupil understands to what extent they have achieved the learning goals, in what way they have achieved them and what has helped them achieve them. From what is said or written they should have a clear idea of where to proceed.

Timing of feedback

With regards to the *when*, Dylan Wiliam (2009) distinguishes between three time frames of feedback: the 'long cycle' (pupils' progress over a year or more), the 'medium cycle' (progress over one to four weeks, which can inform teachers' practices), and the 'short cycle' (the minute-to-minute day-by-day assessments being made during lessons). According to Wiliam, it is the latter cycle that has the potential to have the greatest impact on pupil learning – and therefore on their motivation: 'If students leave the classroom before teachers have used the information about their students' achievements to adjust their teaching, the teachers are already playing catch-up. If the teachers have not made adjustments by the time the students arrive the next day, it is probably too late' (p. 11). This ties in with what one junior school teacher said:

> Immediate feedback is through the lesson. As children are working on their work and you have to focus, there's a lot that goes on with the children talking, and their teacher and the TAs talking, to help them develop. But there's no record of that.

Case study 5.8: The advantages of minute-by-minute assessment

Mr Kneasden and Miss Mapleton are not only poles apart in their approach to behaviour and discipline, but they approach feedback very differently as well. Both are teaching long division to a year 7 maths set. They are using what the school calls the 'bus queue' method to teach it. Both use pictures with a bus stop on the left of the frame and people queuing one behind the other to the right of the stop. They tell the children that this is just like the numbers in a long division exercise. Just as the person nearest the bust stop gets on the bus first, so the number on the left side of the division is the first to be divided. They give instructions to the class, give out the work and tell the pupils they have twenty minutes to do the task. But here the similarity ends. For the next twenty minutes, Mr Kneasden sits at his desk marking another class's work. He makes no attempt to interact with the pupils. At the end of the lesson he collects their books, takes them back to the staff room and sets them aside to mark later. He will not teach that class for another two days. Miss Mapleton, on the other hand, circulates round the class, discussing what the pupils are doing, asking them questions to find out their level of understanding and answering questions they have about the activity.

In both classes a good number of pupils have not really understood the concept of long division. Miss Mapleton discovers this during the course of the lesson and teaches it again to groups of pupils. She makes sure she is giving feedback which helps them learn.

Mr Kneasden does not find out until he marks the books that evening that most pupils have got the answers wrong because they do not understand what to do. He plans to teach it again the next lesson, but, in Wiliam's terms, he is 'already playing catch up'. His pupils have spent a whole lesson being confused and, when they come to the next lesson, Mr Kneasden has not only to begin again from scratch, he also has to try to overcome their anxieties and worries about the maths they are being asked to do. Having 'failed' once, many are not motivated to have another go.

In contrast, the pupils in Miss Mapleton's class have had their confusions recognised during the course of the lesson and the feedback they have received has been very specific and tailored to their needs. They have learned the mathematical concepts bit by bit.

As the teacher quoted above said, there is no written record of the discussions held between Miss Mapleton and her class. The evidence is in the progress they have made in their learning, in their increased confidence to do the task, and in their motivation to learn more. Mr Kneasden may have more in writing, in that his marking points out the mistakes made by the pupils, but his lack of immediate feedback has actually had a negative effect on the learning and the motivation of the pupils in his maths set.

Marking

Feedback from teachers is given verbally and also in written form, through marking. Written feedback given to pupils over a period of time is likely to be of different types, some of which could be said to be 'formative' but, as can be seen from the following examples, much of it is not formative because it does not tell the children how they can improve or make progress in their learning. This is not to say that any feedback that is not strictly 'formative' is a waste of time – it is simply to say that 'feedback' is a complex concept.

Feedback can take many forms:

- Self-feedback, whereby the pupils make comments or reflections regarding their work (e.g. 'I give myself 4 out of 5 because most of it was good but I didn't explain it completely').
- Presentation feedback, whereby the teacher's comments relate to how the work is set out rather than its content (e.g. 'Could be neater').
- Dialogue feedback, a written conversation between pupil and teacher (e.g. Teacher: 'Use a dictionary, please, to make sure all spellings are correct.' Pupil: 'I will try to do it next time.').
- Comment feedback, such as teacher stand-alone written statements (e.g. 'Fab letter well done!').
- Corrective feedback whereby the teacher points out or corrects errors, asking for further information (e.g. 'Can you rewrite this sentence, as it doesn't make sense?').
- Strategic feedback: teachers' comments enable pupils to recognise specific strengths and weaknesses about their work. Strategies are suggested to implement in future work which will lead them towards achieving specified learning goals (e.g. 'Well done for starting with a connective but you have used "as" before. Now think of a different connective to start your sentences.').
- Exemplar/modelling feedback, whereby the teacher gives examples as to how pupils could have gone about the task, showing correct or improved responses to the task (e.g. 'As it trickled over the jagged rocks it sounded like . . .').

Teachers' views

Teachers spend a lot of time marking books – it is not always easy! They need to be convinced it is worthwhile. Here are some comments made by two junior school teachers about their marking and the feedback they give to pupils through that marking.

DANIEL:

> I think when you look at a piece of work, you kind of look at it in two different ways. I think the first way is you look at it from the child's point of view, and you think, 'Has that child done what they're capable of doing? Have they pushed themselves? Have they included the features that you wanted them to? Have they done all that they could for that piece of work?' And then, you look at it from another point of view, which is, 'Here's a list of criteria that will give that child a certain level.' And you use that to try and give them a level. So I think that there are two different ways, because a child might get a low level but they've really put their heart into it, whereas someone else might

have got a high level but have not really worked hard at all. That's when what you write can have an impact on motivation. If a child really has worked hard, you need to acknowledge that and praise them for their effort, even if they did not get it all right. They need to know that you realise how hard they've worked. I think that motivates them to want to keep at it.

I think that's the difference as well, going back to those that achieve higher levels – it's the ones that are willing to go back, to look at their work, respond to it, check it, think, 'Right, is that good?' And I think that's why you need to set up at the beginning what a good bit of work is, so a child knows what to correct. I try to be very clear: 'This is how to be successful. This is what a good piece of work looks like, and this is what makes it good.' I think it's those sorts of pupils that tend to be more motivated to learn. They want their work to be good. Other children just want to get it out of the way.

Daniel's last comment – about the necessity of pupils being shown what a 'good' piece of work looks like – corresponds to something one of the key writers on formative assessment, D. Royce Sadler, wrote a good few years ago. Sadler (1989 p. 129) wrote about teachers' 'guild knowledge' needing to be communicated to pupils in a way that they, too, take on board this 'guild knowledge'. By 'guild knowledge', he was referring to medieval guilds (such as goldsmiths, blacksmiths or fletchers) in which apprentices were taught by masters the 'tricks of their trade'. An apprentice eventually had to produce his own 'masterpiece' in order to become a master himself. The masters passed on to the apprentices their 'guild knowledge', so that the apprentices could judge for themselves what a good piece of work was like. Sadler applies this to school classrooms, and Daniel seems to take this point up.

JUDITH:

I give lots of feedback in their marking, and they're meant to respond to that and they do respond to that. I give feedback throughout the lesson, looking and talking or working with them verbally, but then at the end of every lesson, we mark their work, and I think our marking's quite good. It's thorough. We look at the aim, relating it back to that. Anything you give, whether it's an extra comment, something to develop on, we're always expecting a response from them, so the next lesson they spend the first five, ten minutes responding to our marking. It's really important for them to see that you've been interested in what they've done. I think it's really important. They open that book and they see that you've marked it, that you're concerned about what they've done and they've either had praise for that or they've got some area for development.

Discussion points

a. What are the main points regarding feedback given by these teachers?
b. Why do you think their feedback would be effective?
c. Why do you think it might not achieve what they want it to?

What does feedback mean to the pupils?

These pupils talk about what they think feedback is and what happens when they receive feedback from teachers:

Victoria: They write notes on our work, what we need to do next, what we need to improve – like, if someone needs to improve their handwriting they have to try and do neater handwriting next time.

Alfred: And then she tells us what to improve.

Sarah: Feedback means when you've written something and then you look back to see what the teacher's feedback [is]: 'Well done, remember to start your sentences with adjectives.' That's helpful, so you know what to do next time.

Benjamin: When you've done a piece of work, you don't know if you've done it right or not. And then the feedback helps you. If you get 'Well done, excellent work', then you get really pleased because you know that you've done well. And you'll try to do that again.

THE GOOD THINGS ABOUT FEEDBACK ARE:

Dawn: Talking with teachers about your work is good because they explain what you have to do. The teachers know more so they can help you.

Anne: I like the way teachers write in your books and they put in words that you might want to use, like I had one to use more drop clauses 'cos I wasn't using them as much as I should have done. After that I started using them, my writing got better.

Jane: And it's really like useful because you know what you need to do the next time you do it.

Philip: You could get feedback, then you could jot it down somewhere in your book and then you could look back at that, and go, 'Have I included that in my work?' and, if no, change something about your work.

OTHER PUPILS EXPERIENCED FEEDBACK IN A VERY DIFFERENT WAY:

Ruth: There's people who are actually quite clever and they get 'Good work', but they don't get told *what's* good. Teachers are quite good for saying what's *wrong*, but when it comes to what's good they can't figure it out and they'll just say 'That's really good work'.

Thomas: On the good days, they'll say, like, 'Great, but you should probably work on your description' if you've just done lots and lots of dialogue or something. But they would do that not very many times. They might do it once a week or something. Normally, it would be like 'Try harder'.

FEEDBACK CAN BE EMOTIONAL:

William: You think you've done really well, then you get crushed.

Katherine: Yeah, 'cos the teacher's said, 'Spelling's wrong, try to use more vocabulary.' You've really tried your hardest and it just really upsets you. You feel like you've just done totally really wrong and you've tried your actual hardest.

Henry: If you're really proud of something, and then the teachers says, 'Well, you could improve that', then you feel quite sad because you might be really, that's your best part, and then they say your worst part is your best part. I just went along with it really.

Charlotte: We don't really say, but we just go along with it 'cos the teacher knows more than we do.

Mary: I feel I've done a whole page and then I put my heart into it and the teacher would go and put, like, blah blah blah and stuff like that. I'm embarrassed about it. I feel, like, quite down, because I feel I've put all my heart into it, trying to do that and then they just went and say something bad. But I'd still follow it, but I still feel a bit down because they said something bad about it.

Discussion points

a. How would you account for the great range of response from pupils regarding feedback?

b. To what extent do you think these pupils' views indicate they have experienced genuine assessment for learning?

c. With regard to the different types of written feedback illustrated above, what message does each type of feedback convey to the pupils? What is the message meant to convey (i.e. what does the teacher intend)? What does the message actually convey (i.e. from the pupils' perspective)? For instance, Katherine said that the message she received was that her spellings were no good and this demotivated her. The teacher, hopefully, did not intend this to be the effect at all – she simply wanted Katherine to improve her spellings. This could be an argument for pupil conferencing over giving written feedback through marking.

d. How do you think a pupil's motivation to learn might have been affected by his or her various experiences of assessment?

Peer and self-assessment

AfL is not an easy option for pupils. It demands that they become reflective learners who take responsibility for their own learning. In order to be fully effective, pupils need to become participants in the learning process rather than simply recipients of it. Part of encouraging active participation in the learning process is that pupils are asked to assess their own work. This can be very threatening if it is not something they are used to. In order to be able to effectively assess themselves, pupils need to be given specific training:

*   to recognise and understand the learning objectives of lessons;
*   to know and understand the success criteria for those lessons; and
*   on how to make use of the time given for self-assessment.

Pupils are also asked to assess each other – to participate in peer assessment. In order to do this, pupils need to know how to give constructive feedback to their peers.

Case study 5.9: Peer assessment

Mrs Crowther's literacy lesson is drawing to a close. The pupils have had twenty minutes to write their sequence of events in their books. She tells them to stop writing and asks the class to come to the carpet with their literacy books. She asks the class to read what they have written to whomever they are sitting next to. The pupil listening is asked to check what has been written against the Remember To points which are still on the interactive whiteboard. The pupils begin to talk with each other, and the noise level increases in the class dramatically. One pupil, Simon, is sitting right in the middle of the group. He has pupils all around him, but they have all paired off – he has no one to read to. He looks around the room at what others are doing, then back to his own book which is on his lap. Mrs Crowther asks the pupils to tick where they have met the Remember To points. They are then to put their books on the top of the cupboard at the back of the class so that she can mark them at the end of the day. Simon has had no one to read with, but he puts his book away with the rest.

This is an example of a short period of peer assessment. In this case, the pupils were asked to talk with each other about their work and to try to see to what extent the other had met the success criteria for the lesson. For most children, this works – but, for Simon, there is a problem. For whatever reason, he has no one with whom to pair off.

Peer assessment – pupils working in groups or with partners to review and reflect on each other's work – is a key aspect of AfL. Like self-assessment, it is something that needs to be taught and practised. For some pupils, this can be the most threatening aspect of AfL. It is one thing to have the teacher or teaching assistant look at your work and it is OK to be asked to review it yourself, but to expose your work to your friends (or otherwise) in the class is something else. For other pupils, like Simon, it can be the cause of embarrassment and distress. Much will depend on the climate being established in the class and school as a whole. Peer assessment cannot be introduced in isolation from everything else to do with AfL.

What the pupils say about peer assessment

GETTING OTHER PUPILS' OPINIONS:

Dawn: We mark each other's, sometimes. We swap books and write what we think, like which things we think are good about it and which things we *don't* think are so good. You get other people's opinions and not just the teacher's and they explain things better than the teacher sometimes – you can understand what they say.

WHAT IS DIFFICULT ABOUT PEER ASSESSMENT?

Linda: Sometimes, when I'm marking someone else's books, sometimes they do something that doesn't make sense. But if you write 'This doesn't make sense, I don't think you should include this in your work', then you might think that would make them sad. So then you feel *bad* – sometimes it's hard marking other people's work, 'cos you think they're going to be upset.

Matthew: We are asked, sometimes, to swap books with each other and write comments about how well they did and highlight, say, their best word or sentence. I feel bad if I put bad stuff about their work, so I mainly write about the good things.

WHAT IS USEFUL ABOUT PEER ASSESSMENT?

Matthew: When we mark each other's work we understand how the teacher marked *ours*.
Philip: Yeah, may be in literacy you could say to your partner, 'Please can you read this and give me some feedback on it. Is it good or bad? What should I add?' So if you get feedback from the person, they're kind of helping you and saying, 'Ooh, you could have improved on that' or something. And this is what the teacher does too.

IT IS IMPORTANT WHICH PUPILS DO THE PEER ASSESSMENT

Esther: I don't mind doing it because I sit next to Ahmed and he's the same level as me. So I think that if *I* make a mistake, then he wouldn't laugh because he's the same level. And if *he* makes a mistake then he knows that I wouldn't laugh, because we're at the same level, and also 'cos he's one of my friends.

PUPILS NEED TO BE TAUGHT HOW TO ASSESS EACH OTHER'S WORK

Simon: It's difficult because you don't know what's *bad* and what's *good*. 'Cos you're looking through the work and you can't see anything bad, but the teacher might say, 'put all the good things about them and the bad things about them', but you don't know what to *do* 'cos you can't see any bad things.
Nathan: It *is* actually quite hard to mark other people's work.

There is clearly a role for the teacher and teaching assistant to monitor peer assessment and to give guidance on what to look out for and how to highlight aspects which achieve the aims of the lesson and which aspects could be improved. Perhaps pupils can be taught the 'evaluation sandwich' (see p. 106). If peer assessment is to help motivate pupils to learn, then it must be done properly.

Summary

In this chapter we have looked at:

- Types of assessment, summative, formative, diagnostic and dynamic.
- Strategies (clear learning aims and success criteria, feedback and self and peer appraisal) which need to be applied consistently in order for AfL to be effective.
- How AfL can only facilitate pupil motivation to learn if it is delivered in the context of an understanding, positive, learning environment by teachers who really know what they are doing.

Chapter 6

Moving forward together

An overview

This chapter focuses on everyday dilemmas experienced in the classroom by teachers and teaching assistants engaged in motivating pupils to learn and behave. While numerous theories have been presented in this book, this particular chapter will illustrate how theory and research can be applied to everyday situations and that teaching assistants and teachers working together can achieve more than either working individually.

Common pupil responses: 'I won't, but I could'

Ms Blunt (teacher) and Jo (TA) were discussing coursework for the year 10 music class, and both were at their wits' end regarding what to do with Miles. It all started with the following conversation:

Jo: It is not that Miles is not able. In fact, he is very able.
Ms Blunt: He has flair and potential, he is just not motivated.
Jo: Yesterday, he asked me why he had to learn the difference between a major and a minor chord.
Ms Blunt: And what did you say?
Jo: 'Because you need to be able to do it for your assessment, you have to do it.' Frankly, I just told him to get on with it.
Ms Blunt: That's the problem, not only with Miles but many of the others in the class. They *could* do it, but they don't see the relevance, the point . . . They don't see how it relates to their future, their personal goals and they don't feel they have any choice.

Ms Blunt and Jo reflected on various motivational theories. To begin with, they considered that motivation is highest when pupils feel competent, have sufficient autonomy, set worthwhile goals and receive constructive feedback. Ms Blunt and Jo then looked at theories regarding regulation and self-regulation (see pp. 61–62). These theories discussed the importance of setting challenging goals and argued that motivation resulted from pupils being given choices as to their involvement in the task. Motivation should be highest when pupils have some involvement in the why, how, when, where, what and with whom the task should be completed.

The conversation between Ms Blunt and Jo continued.

Ms Blunt: It is difficult to know what to say to pupils when they ask why do I have to do this, or they tell you 'It's not as if I want to become a musician.' For some pupils, telling them they have to do this in order to earn a good grade is enough. Some pupils are motivated to get good grades and learn material that they may not find personally interesting because they see the end goal in sight. They realise that good GCSEs lead to good 'A' levels and a chance to go to university. On the other hand, some pupils just do what they are told to in order to please the teacher or to keep out of trouble – but what we really want is to develop in the pupils an internalised thirst for knowledge.

Jo: We want to encourage pupils to do the task because they want to, not because they have to – but how?

Ms Blunt: The pupils need to feel in control.

Jo: But we're in control.

Ms Blunt: It is the *perception* of control that is important. We will give them a choice of three tasks to be assessed at the end of the half term and tell them that these tasks will correspond to the areas of performing, composing and appraising. We will also give them an option of working individually or in small groups and an option of how to present the assignment; that is, they could do an individual performance or a PowerPoint presentation.

Jo: That's sounds great, but pupils will need to know how they will be marked. Some will ask 'What do I need to do to get a certain level?' If pupils are comfortable with doing one type of assignment, then they often get confused with doing another type of assignment – they just don't know what is expected of them.

Ms Blunt: Yes, we need to make the assessment criteria clear. Understanding the assessment criteria will enable the pupils to feel that they are in control of their grade – they will know what they need to do to achieve a certain grade.

Jo: It has to be pupil friendly so that the pupils understand. I also need to understand, so that I can help the pupils to understand.

Ms Blunt: Ok, we will go over this.

Jo: Getting back to Miles: I think part of the difficulty Miles faces is that he gets bored. Miles needs to feel that the subject is personally relevant to him.

Ms Blunt: Possibly we need to rethink our reward policy. Currently, we reward those pupils who achieve the highest grades, but perhaps will need to think of rewarding those pupils who achieve a grade that matches his or her target grade.

Jo: So, shall I sit down with Miles and talk to him about what he wants to achieve; that is, get him to set a personal challenge that would hopefully motivate him to engage in the task?

Ms Blunt: Yes. Also, you could discuss with him what he would see as a suitable reward; that is, how he would choose to reward himself for meeting and achieving his personal challenge. Remember, we are trying to help pupils to become intrinsically motivated.

In this example, in trying to engage a pupil who 'won't' do the task but 'could' do the task, the key to moving forward was giving choices, making assessment criteria clear and changing the reward policy for the assignments. Of course, this dilemma – of a pupil who 'won't but could' – could be handled in a number of ways. How would you work with such a pupil using motivational theory?

Common pupil responses: 'I can't' – the pupil who could, but thinks she would just die if she failed

The trouble with Amy is not a question of ability. Amy is a very bright girl, but she is so afraid of failing that she dissolves into tears whenever faced with a new task or situation.

Mr Calloway: What can we do about Amy?

Sadie: She just falls apart whenever I ask her to do a task. I gave her the maths sheet to work on today and she just said 'I can't do it', and ripped it up.

Mr Calloway: The point is that she *can* do it but she thinks she can't. I am always telling her that she can do it, but she just does not listen. And what is really difficult to understand is that when she does do the work she always gets top marks.

Sadie: When I sit with her, we go over it stage by stage but, as soon as we get to a bit that she finds difficult, she just freezes.

Mr Calloway: Amy is an extreme example, but there are other pupils in the class who are terrified of trying in case they try and fail.

Sadie: I was talking to Amy's mum the other day and she said Amy is like that at home and always has been.

Mr Calloway: Of course, there are those pupils who fear failure to such a great degree that not trying is the safer option. If they do not try, and fail, they can always say to themselves, 'I failed because I did not try'.

The problem with Amy and other pupils who are paralysed by the fear of failure is what they say to themselves; in a manner of speaking, they are their own worst enemy. This behaviour can be understood in terms of the powerful motivation to avoid failure (p. 32), attribution theory (pp. 34–36), self-handicapping behaviour (p. 41) and goal orientation, i.e. whether the pupil has learning or performance goals (pp. 56–60). One way of moving forward is to make various ways of thinking regarding failure explicit to the pupil, challenge these ways of thinking and to model more adaptive ways of thinking regarding how to respond to challenging learning situations. Responding to this challenge, the teacher, Mr Calloway, suggests a role play activity.

The role play event

Mr Calloway: Right, Sadie, remember what we discussed and planned last night. I am going to give you some work and you are going to come up with all sorts of reasons why you cannot do it. Ok, I'm going to call the class together. Right, class – now what I want to talk about is the project. I will give you a few choices regarding what you can do. As we are talking about the Victorians, you could choose a project on Victorian children, the Victorian school, Victorian working life or Victorian factory workers.

Sadie: I would choose the topic 'Victorian school'.

Mr Calloway: Why is that, Sadie?

Sadie: Well it is something that I already know a lot about – and, no, it is not because I went to a Victorian school.

Mr Calloway: Well that is interesting, but I am curious. Why do you want to do a project about something you already know?

Sadie: Well, if I am very honest, I like people to think I am clever, and if I choose something I already know about then it will be really easy to get a top grade and then everybody will see how clever I am.

(Children laugh.)

Mr Calloway: But, Sadie! The purpose of having a choice of what project to do is to choose something that you find interesting, but the *main reason* for working on a project is to find out information that you don't already know. Doing a project is a great opportunity to learn something new.

Sadie: Well, I am interested in Victorian factory workers, but I don't know anything about that and I want to get an A.

Mr Calloway: I don't see the problem.

Sadie: But it will be hard and I might not get a good grade.

Mr Calloway: But it is not so much about the grade you get but whether you have done your personal best.

Sadie: But it is about the grade. If I don't get the top marks, if I make a mistake, people will laugh and think I'm dumb.

Mr Calloway: I won't think you're dumb. Who would think you are dumb?

Sadie: You don't get it! The worst thing that could happen would be for me to really try and then to fail.

Mr Calloway: Sadie, everyone likes to get a good grade, but what is more important is that you do your personal best. As long as you do your personal best and you learn, you are successful.

Sadie: But I hate to fail. I hate to get things wrong. If I don't try, then I won't get things wrong.

Mr Calloway: Making mistakes is not easy, but you cannot learn if you do not make mistakes. If you don't try, you will never know what you can really achieve.

This conversation was just the beginning of many dialogues that Sadie and Mr Calloway had with the class about learning, doing your personal best and facing your personal demons i.e. the fear of failure. Did it make a difference?

Mr Calloway reflects that, slowly, these strategies were beginning to make an impact. As Mr Calloway said to Sadie, telling the class about the value of learning and how learning involves making mistakes is the first step. The real challenge is getting the pupils to say these positive self-statements to themselves. It is important that, when pupils attempt personally challenging tasks or mastery attempts, they need to be praised. Now, when pupils such as Amy are hesitant about starting challenging work, Mr Calloway and Sadie make a point of saying, 'If you don't try you will never know whether you can do the task' and that, in Mr Calloway's class, students are always rewarded for trying personally challenging tasks. Of course, there is always the issue of knowing what is personally challenging for any individual pupil. For this, he relies on his professional judgment, the insightful reflections of Sadie, his TA, and the growing self-awareness of his pupils.

Common pupil responses: 'I don't need to' – the pupil who is not ready to change

This type of pupil is well known to staff members, as they always seem to be in trouble. This conversation takes place between Jason, Head of Pastoral Support, and Lynne, an LSA.

Jason: I can't remember how many times I have met with Todd about his behaviour: Todd skipping lessons; Todd kicking off in classes and being taken out of lessons; Todd punching other pupils. But every time I meet with him, Todd's standard reply is that it is not his fault. In fact, everyone else is to blame except him. Todd potentially is an able pupil, but he does not realise that if he does not get down to work he will leave this school with no GCSEs.

Lynne: In my role supporting Todd, we have had numerous conversations and he does promise me that next time will be different, that he will show up for English and that he will behave in Mr Sahid's science class, but then it's just the same. I think he makes the promises just to keep me quiet and that he has no intention to change.

Jason: That's just it – Todd does not think he needs to change.

This example deals with a pupil who needs to find the motivation to change and engage in learning. This situation can best be understood within a framework of motivational interviewing (see p. 53) which builds upon a model of change (Prochaska and DiClemente 1982) that sees change as a process.

Jason (Head of Pastoral Support) and Lynne (Todd's LSA) attend a number of training sessions on motivational interviewing techniques and subsequently put into place an action plan. They then meet to discuss Todd's progress:

Jason: From my point of view, a key factor in motivational interviewing is to have the pupil realise that his behaviour is pushing him further and further away from his long terms goals. It is not enough that we say it but, in order for real change to occur, Todd must come to this realisation for himself.

Lynne: And of course Todd is always talking about how he wants to become a plumber. He is hoping to take a course at college and move to Australia.

Jason: I sat down with Todd last week and I asked him what he wanted to do in the future and he mentioned the plumbing course and then I asked him what he needed to do to actually get on that course and what he actually needed to be doing right now to enable him to make his dreams come true. I think that really made Todd think.

Lynne: I had a discussion with Todd last week about his being kicked out of Mr Sahid's science class. And, to begin with, it was the usual, 'Miss, it was not my fault', 'Sir is always picking on me' and 'I didn't do nothing wrong'. I got Todd to draw a timeline backwards so to speak, starting with being kicked out and then moving backwards to the original incident that triggered his outburst. For Todd, this was having another pupil throw a pen at him. I asked him if he had a choice in regard to how he acted towards that pupil and how other pupils would react. Todd admitted that most other pupils would be annoyed, but they would not have punched the other pupil. I asked Todd what would happen if, as a plumber, he got annoyed with his boss and hit him. I think Todd is beginning to think more about his behaviour and is realising that he needs to change his behaviour.

Jason: I think Todd is moving from the precontemplation stage, in which he does not think that there is a problem, to the contemplation stage in which he realises that his behaviour is causing him to suffer. Hopefully, Todd will next move to the determinism stage in which he will start to actively work towards changing his behaviour.

Lynne: About our discussions with Todd: you getting him to think about future goals, and myself getting Todd to think about the causes of his actions and other choices he could have made, are key to moving his thinking forward.

Jason: I think, in our discussions with him, it is the language that we use that is so important. We must totally believe that change is possible for him. If we doubt his potential to change then he will begin to doubt it as well.

Lynne: I agree. Talking to his parents would be a helpful next step. Though they want the best for Todd, his mother can be negative. From her point of view she has heard it all before. And, of course, we need to talk to his teachers. Mr Sahid, the science teacher, is fed up with Todd and, though he is professional enough not to say that in so many words, the way he looks at Todd when he enters the room says it all.

Jason: I'll talk to Mr Sahid. Our beliefs about the possibility of our pupils changing can become a self-fulfilling prophecy. In fact, conducting training for all staff in regard to motivational interviewing techniques the model of change would be really beneficial.

In this case, the Head of Pastoral Support and the LSA working together were instrumental in starting the change process for one pupil. Of course, the process of change is not easy.

Lynne: I was really so pleased with Todd's progress. Todd seemed really motivated to change. He was attending classes and doing his work and then he just lost it last Friday, in Mr Sahid's science class.

Jason: Yes – truly a disappointing setback. But we must remember that part of the change cycle is to have the occasional relapse and what is crucial is that Todd gets back on track.

Lynne: I had a talk with Todd this morning, and he is really disappointed in his behaviour and he feels that he has let himself down.

Jason: What we do not want is for Todd to give up.

Lynne: Todd is not going to do that. I don't know if you know this, but I have been using this process of change on myself to finally give up smoking. I have been talking to Todd about this and when he was talking about his relapse in the science class I was talking about my relapse at my friend's 40th birthday party on the weekend. Funnily enough, both of us talking about how we felt when we had failed made us both feel better and more determined to get back on the programme.

Jason: Well done! That is the real advantage with this model of change. Change is hard and slow but using this model you can see progress. Also, I think your relationship with Todd is key. You really care about Todd's progress and he realises that. Well done!

Common pupil responses: 'I can't, I really can't' – the pupil who does not have the underlying skills

There are many reasons why pupils are not motivated to try to engage in learning, and one obvious one is that the pupil actually does not have the necessary underlying skills. In the following situation, we return to Ms Smythe and Josie, who are discussing pupil progress in chemistry.

Josie: With all due respect, revising the periodic table is not interesting.

Ms Smythe: Yes, but they do have to know it for their exam. Ok, we could talk about how to get the pupils to revise, but what I am concerned with is the progress of many of the pupils

Josie: Many of them will fail the exam if they do not revise.

Ms Smythe: But we don't want them to fail. And, of course, there are many reasons for their behaviour.

Josie: But for many of them that is all that they get: more and more failing grades. I think that is why many of them misbehave, and are totally disrespectful. Who can blame them for giving up and mucking about?

Ms Smythe: But why are they failing? That is where it gets complex. I think for some their family life is so dysfunctional that they are not in an emotional state to learn and that at best what we can do is provide is security.

Josie: Do you mean that we should have lower expectations for them?

Ms Smythe: No, we need to have high expectations for all pupils – they all need to strive for their personal best.

Josie: Part of the problem, as I see it, is that they are not doing the revision work because they are simply not able. They have not been paying attention in class and they simply do not have the notes from which to revise, nor the skills to comprehend the textbook.

Ms Smythe: I think, Josie, it has been helpful to have this discussion with you and it is clear that we need to think about how we will work with the class together. We will meet and discuss this in greater detail tomorrow.

For Josie and Mrs Smythe, the first step forward in meeting the learning needs of the class was to have an honest and constructive discussion regarding what they thought were the issues and how they could move forward. After having this honest constructive conversation, both felt more positive and less stressed about their working relationship.

Ms Smythe: Let's first think of the pupils who do not have the underlying skills that they need.

Josie: What we need to do is to return to basics; to give them the essential knowledge they need. But we need to do it in a way that does not single them out as being behind. Also, many of them don't know how to revise – I didn't know how to, at their age.

Ms Smythe: I suppose the truth is that many of the pupils in this class, for many different reasons, just don't have the necessary skills to start revision so they are therefore not motivated to work. In a sense, they are engaging in self-handicapping behaviour: they know they don't know, but if they try and then fail, it is obvious to everyone that they don't know. However, if they muck around then they will fail, but they can say to themselves, 'I have failed because I haven't tried'.

Josie: We can make revision notes for them.

Ms Smythe: I can make revision notes for them, but then *I* am doing the revising and they will not learn how to make revision notes themselves. They need to become independent learners. Certainly, by this age they need to be developing these skills. We will go over the basics. I will divide the class into groups, so that in every group there is a group leader who should be able to remember some basic facts, and part of his or her role is to teach the other group members. We will not only be teaching them basic facts about chemistry but we need to teach them basic facts about how to revise.

Josie: We also need to make the activity fun.

Ms Smythe: You say 'fun', but I would like to say 'engaging'.

Josie: How about we use music? I know that many of the class are part of the school's Glee Club. Perhaps they could learn the periodic table by setting the key facts to some song – rap song or mash up – if they want. Also, there are pupils in the class who are struggling at science but are very talented at music. In this way, they will be able to demonstrate to the other pupils and us that they are talented and have value. If they then feel good about themselves, perhaps they will feel more motivated to try to learn the material.

Ms Smythe: Good idea. That is what an inclusive class should be – appreciating the value of all pupils. I also think we need to engage their curiosity. I will ask them all to come up with questions they want to know about science and we will have a few moments in each lesson to discuss a question they wish to have answered so that, hopefully, they will see the value and relevance of science.

What this scenario illustrates is that, in any one class, the reasons for not engaging in learning can be complex – but sometimes a lack of motivation to engage is due to a pupil simply not having the necessary skills and the confidence to try.

Research in action: working with children who are anxious and angry, in order to remove barriers to learning and develop emotional resilience

The next scenario explores how a group of schools, with support from CAMHS (Child and Adolescent Mental Health Services), developed an innovative programme that looked at how children responded to learning challenges. The project team included a lead head teacher, an educational psychologist, a primary mental health worker, a CAMHS commissioner and a specialist behaviour teacher. At the outset, all children in the programme were lacking the motivation to engage; however, the pupils' reasons for not engaging differed.

The pilot project

Fifteen schools with pupils aged 5–13 worked together to improve the emotional well-being of their pupils. Resilience within the project was defined as that which 'enables one to survive and function, despite disadvantage and risk beyond the normal challenges of growing up' (Masten 2001). Public health data had indicated that this should be a priority and head teachers identified a significant number of pupils who struggled daily to engage in learning, and therefore required a targeted approach.

The project aimed to develop an approach that intervened early with children who experienced challenges in learning situations. Children were identified as either:

- 'internalising-withdrawn, anxious children' who in the classroom are fearful of new things without reason, believing they can't do what they are capable of, and who are often unresponsive and unable to enjoy activities, and who struggling to socialise and work collaboratively; or
- 'externalising-acting out, angry children' who in the classroom have a short attention span, are often out of their seat, disturb their peers, are verbally challenging to teachers and teaching assistants or ignore them, and disrupt group work by arguing and not being able to collaborate.

The project described

The fifteen schools sent two teaching assistants and a lead teacher to three professional development days, at which staff learned about the psychology of resilience and impacting psycho-social aspects in the classroom. The outcome of the project was to have children who could say:

'*I am* likeable and respect myself and others.'

'*I can* find ways to solve problems and control myself.'

'*I have people* to love me and help me.'

In each participating school, teaching assistants and teachers together identified pupils in need of further support. To identify pupils, a resilience checklist was used, which assessed a child's ability:

- to recognise and express emotions appropriately
- to regulate difficult emotions such as anxiety or disappointment

- to see things from another's perspective
- to be able to master a skill
- to believe that you 'can do it'
- to develop and use active coping strategies
- to problem solve
- to help and support
- to make plans and set goals
- to make successful relationships in school.

Together, teachers and TAs considered the abilities of the children in their classes. If children demonstrated only a few of these abilities consistently, or if they were unable to demonstrate any abilities, they were considered for group work which aimed to develop these competencies. The final decision on group composition also included consideration of group dynamics; for example, a mixture of externalising and internalising pupils. Together, teachers and teaching assistants, in their school groups, planned how to use the SEAL Silver set materials. The sets used were 'Good to be Me' and 'Going for Goals'. Each school planned its programme with support from the trainers, and based it on knowledge of its pupils. Each child in the group completed a 'Kid Cope' questionnaire (Spirito et al. 1988) before the sessions started. This informed staff of areas that the children found particularly challenging and strategies that the children did not or rarely used to manage situations. The sessions ran weekly.

In one school, a Key Stage 2 group was called 'Life Explorers'. The first six sessions were based on the 'Good to be Me' materials, and in each session a skill or strategy was developed that was printed on a card that got added to a key ring over the weeks. The pupils were encouraged to keep this in their pockets so as to remind them of strategies during the school day. These cards, which became personal reminders, included:

- I am good at . . .
- I can talk about my achievements . . .
- I know I am not the only person who has worries . . .
- It's OK to feel frightened and upset . . .
- I can recognise when I begin to become upset . . .
- I can find ways to chill . . .

Activities included making angry balloons filled with water and covered with words about what made them angry that were then thrown at the wall, and a range of relaxation techniques. At the end of the sessions, the children each made a medal and gave it to someone else, explaining why they that person should receive it.

At the end of the programme, the Kid Cope questionnaire was repeated, and it was found that pupils were now more confident in managing their worries and frustrations without becoming anxious, disengaging or acting out. Staff also noticed that pupils were calmer and more able to learn in class.

Impact

Results from the schools in the project showed that there was a significant increase in the use of positive active coping strategies in Key Stage 1 and Key Stage 2, particularly related to social support, emotional regulation, problem solving and cognitive restructuring and, at

Key Stage 3, with emotional regulation. There was a decrease in use of negative strategies (particularly in relation to criticism of others) at Key Stage 1 and in criticism of others and self- criticism at Key stage 2 and 3. Referrals to specialist CAMHS from the schools were reduced during the period of the project by 20 per cent compared with the previous year. Head teachers across the locality reported less exclusions, better attendance, improved engagement in learning and raised attainment.

As an example, the impact of the project on an 'internalising' (withdrawn, anxious child) was described by the child as:

- Now I have started to say what I think and feel to an adult in the classroom.
- Before, I would worry all afternoon if my Mum would collect me on time. I have realised now [that] my Mum will come even if she is late, and having a book helps me to wait.
- I don't worry so much about my family in class, and so I get my work done quicker.

As an example, the impact on an 'externalising' (acting out, angry child) was described by the child as resulting in the following:

- I listen to my teaching assistant more. I know she cares about me.
- I try not to muck about in class, and I have a go at my work if my teaching assistant is nearby to support me.
- Now, when I am angry my teaching assistant reminds me about the relaxation techniques we learned, and I try and practise these so I calm down.

After the pilot project, school staff across the locality reflected on the programme's impact on the children involved. They reported that they now had a greater understanding of children's behaviour and how to engage them in learning. They worked together to outline concrete strategies to use and had developed their understanding of how to support pupils in different situations by, for example, developing a spread sheet of situations and strategies as illustrated in Table 6.1.

At the conclusion of the pilot, teachers and teaching assistants realised that key to the project's success had been:

- Quality professional development days on key aspects of theory and practice, leading to an understanding of why children behave as they do.
- Time to reflect, plan, make decisions and review them together.
- Regular and consistent support for pupils being targeted and time for them to talk to class teachers.
- Professional support from the primary mental health worker, educational psychologist and specialist behaviour teacher.
- Support from the leadership in the school and, more widely, the pilot project being championed across the locality by a lead head teacher.

(Katharine Amaladoss, head teacher, 2011)

Summary

This chapter has looked at a number of situations about pupils who are not motivated to engage in learning or to behave in an appropriate manner in order that they are able to learn. Although on the surface the pupils seem the same, in that they are not engaging, the reason

Table 6.1 Strategies to use

Issue	I used to . . .	Outcome for child	Now I . . .	Outcome for child
The child refuses to engage in a task.	Administer blanket orders and feel frustrated.	Child becomes angry and defiant.	Listen to the child, and their feelings and talk about strategies.	The child attempts work more frequently and is less disruptive.
The child would be very anxious about the day and be unwilling to try.	Feel I was a failure. I would get cross inside that they worried about everything, and then I would do the work for them.	Child becomes dependant and feelings of anxiety are reinforced.	Talk through a visual timetable at the beginning of the day and the strategies that we have learned in the group work, and set task in small steps with lots of encouragement.	The child is less anxious and will 'have a go'.

for the disengagement is crucial in determining what strategies could be most effective in moving them forward. Sometimes teachers and teaching assistants need to change first by adopting different approaches and strategies based on an understanding of motivational theory. Table 6.2 summarises some common pupil responses, with suggested strategies. However, there are many more reasons why pupils choose not to engage and often any behaviour can be explained by a multitude of factors.

Conclusion

A collaborative relationship would entail teachers and teaching assistants finding the time to discuss motivational challenges. It is through discussing complex learning dilemmas that teachers and teaching assistants can spark off ideas in one another and together can discover ways forward. Teaching assistants are an invaluable extra pair of eyes in the classroom and, working together, teachers and teaching assistants can accomplish more than either working individually.

Table 6.2 Types of pupil response with suggested strategies

Type of pupil	Underlying theories that could help to explain the behaviour	Strategies used
'I won't, but I could.'	Regulation and self-regulation (pp. 61–62). Intrinsic/extrinsic motivation (pp. 47–48). Goal orientation (pp. 56–60).	Allowing pupil control and giving choices regarding why, how, when, where, what and with whom the task should be completed. Encouraging learning goals.
'I can't' – the pupil who could, but thinks she would just die if she failed.	Goal orientation (pp. 56–60). Mastery attempts (p. 56). Attribution theory (pp. 34–36). Motivation to avoid failure (p. 32).	Modelling adaptive thinking styles. Praising mastery attempts.
'I don't need to' – the pupil who is not ready to change.	Motivational interviewing techniques (p. 53). Process of change (p. 54).	Encouraging pupils to consider present behaviour in terms of its impact on future goals. Encouraging pupils to examine reasons for their behaviour and consider if they could behave differently. Modelling process of change.
'I can't – I really can't.'	Multiple intelligence theory (pp. 42–43). Self-worth (pp. 40–42). Self-handicapping behaviour (p. 41).	Identifying pupils' strengths in reference to multiple intelligences and using this knowledge to teach other skills. Scaffolding, developing and building skills, but not in a manner that encourages dependence. Breaking complex tasks into smaller bite-size chunks.

Glossary

Attributions How individuals explain to themselves the outcomes of events, for example, why they failed or why they succeeded.

Cognitive evaluation theory states that rewards have the potential to both control and inform.

Deep learning sees learning as changing ourselves. It is a means of finding out and connecting with the reality of the world around us.

Demotivation refers to aspects of the classroom environment or the learning situation that can cancel out even strong existing motivation in pupils.

Effectance motivation assumes that individuals need to feel competent in their interactions with their environment and that this type of motivation leads to 'mastery attempts' (attempting challenging activities).

Extrinsic motivation Pupils whose behaviour is driven by a 'what's in it for me?' attitude are said to be extrinsically motivated; that is, the source of their motivation lies outside themselves.

Goal orientation theory aims to explain how pupils learn and perform in school. There are two distinct approaches, one being a mastery orientation in which the pupil focuses on the process of learning and the other a performance orientation in which the pupil focuses on demonstrating ability, getting good grades and out performing other pupils.

Intrinsic motivation involves engaging in an activity for its own sake.

Mastery goal Also called a learning goal or a task-focused goal, the focus is on improving one's competence through learning new skills and understanding new material.

Motivational interviewing techniques aim to facilitate change by promoting pupil knowledge and concern regarding behaviour to the point at which the pupil sees for him or herself a need for change.

Participation is a term central to Wenger's views of a 'community of practice'. 'Participation' requires the engagement of the whole person (feelings, will and mind), their imagination (a sense of what participants might become) and alignment of their values with the values of the community (the values of the community in practice become my values).

Performance goal Here the focus is on the pupil demonstrating ability, getting good grades and out performing other pupils.

Regulation If a goal or task is regulated, then its progress is monitored and controlled by external forces such as a teacher or teaching assistant telling a pupil why, how, when, where, what and with whom the task should be completed.

Self-regulation refers to the process whereby pupils activate and sustain thought, behaviours and feelings that are geared towards keeping to, and meeting, goals.

Self-worth A person's overall feelings and emotions about themselves as a person.

Surface learning treats learning as something external to the learner; a task to perform, such as gathering facts and information, which is taken in from the outside. Pupils will often engage only in surface learning, for example, in getting a grip on 'facts' which enable them to pass a test, but forgetting these facts soon afterwards.

Unhealthy attributions One type of unhealthy attribution involves having low effort attribution; that is, pupils do not seem to think their effort makes a difference. Another type of unhealthy attribution is where a pupil will attribute successes to external factors that are not in his or her control (known as 'external attribution'). For example, the reason he or she scored a goal was that the wind had blown the ball in.

Bibliography

Alborz, A., Pearson, D., Farrell, P. and Howes, A. (2009) *The Impact of Adult Support Staff on Pupils and Mainstream Schools*, EPPI-Centre, Institute of Education, EPPI-Centre report no. 17021T.

Ames, C. (1992) 'Classrooms, Goals, Structures and Student Motivation', 84 *Journal of Educational Psychology*, pp. 267–71.

Assessment Reform Group (ARG) (2002) *Assessment for Learning: 10 Principles*, London: Institute of Education.

Atkinson, J. W. (1964) *An Introduction to Motivation*, Princeton, NJ: Van Nostrand.

Atkinson, J. W. and Birch, D. (1974) 'The Dynamics of Achievement Orientated Activity', in Atkinson, J. W. and Raynor, J. O. (eds) *Motivation and Achievement*, Washington, DC: Winston and Sons, pp. 271–325.

Balshaw, M. (1999) *Help in the Classroom* (2nd edition), London: David Fulton Publishers.

Bani, M. (2011) 'The Use and Frequency of Verbal and Non-verbal Praise in Nurture Groups', 16(1) *Emotional and Behavioural Difficulties*, pp. 47–67.

Bentham, S. (2011) *An Exploration of Collaborative Relationships between Teachers and Teaching Assistants*, unpublished Institution-Focused Study, Institute of Education, University of London.

Black, P. and Wiliam, D. (1998) 'Assessment and Classroom Learning', 5(1) *Assessment in Education*, pp. 7–63.

Black, P. and Wiliam, D. (2006) 'Assessment for Learning in the Classroom', in Gardner, J. (ed.), *Assessment and Learning*, London: Sage.

Blatchford, P., Bassett, P., Brown, P., Koutsoubou, M., Martin, C., Russell, A., and Webster, R. with Rubie-Davies, C. (2009) *Deployment and Impact of Support Staff in Schools: The Impact of Support Staff in Schools (Results from Strand 2, Wave 2)*, research report no. DCSF-RR148, London: DCSF.

Blatchford, P., Bassett, P., Brown, P., Martin, C., Russell, A., Webster, R., Babayicit, S., and Haywood, N. (2008) *Deployment and Impact of Support Staff in Schools and the Impact of the National Agreement (Results from strand 2, Wave 1)*, 2005/06 report, London: DCSF.

Boaler, J. (1997) 'When Even the Winners Are Losers: Evaluating the Experience of 'Top Set' Students', 29(2) *Journal of Curriculum Studies*, pp. 165–182.

Boaler, J., Wiliam, D. and Brown, M. (2000) 'Students' Experience of Ability Grouping – Disaffection, Polarisation and the Construction of Failure', 26(5) *British Educational Research Journal*, pp. 631–648.

Broadfoot, P. and Black, P. (2004), 'Redefining Assessment? The First Ten Years of Assessment in Education', 11(1) *Assessment in Education: Principles, Policy and Practice*, pp. 7–26.

Brookfield, S. D. (1995) *Becoming a Critically Reflective Teacher*, San Francisco, CA: Jossey-Bass.

Brookhart, S. (2001) 'Successful Students' Formative and Summative Uses of Assessment Information', 8(2) *Assessment in Education: Principles, Policy and Practice*, pp. 153–169.

Bruner, J. (1996) *The Culture of Education*, London: Harvard University Press.

Bubb, S. and Earley, P. (2006) 'Taking Responsibility for Teachers' Professional Learning: the School's Role', paper presented at the University of London and Beijing Normal University International Conference, 3–6 May.

Chapin, M. and Dyck, D. G. (1976) 'Persistence in Children's Reading Length as a Function of N Length and Attribution Retraining', 85 *Journal of Abnormal Psychology*, pp. 511–515.

Chen, C. and Stevenson, H. (1995) 'Motivation and Mathematics Achievement: A Comparative Study of Asian-American, Caucasian-American and East Asian High School Students', 66 *Child Development*, pp. 1214–1234.

Christensen, P. and Prout, A. (2005) 'Anthropological and Sociological Perspectives on the Study of Children', in Greene, S. and Hogan, D. (eds), *Researching Children's Experience*, London: Sage.

Cigman, R. (2006) 'The Gifted Child: A Conceptual Enquiry', 32(2) *Oxford Review of Education*, pp. 197–212.

Cooley, C. H. (1902) *Human Nature and the Social Order*, New York: Scribner.

Corno, L. (1993) 'The Best-laid Plans: Modern Conceptions of Volition and Educational Research', 22(2) *Educational Researcher*, pp. 14–22.

Covington, M. (1992) *Making the Grade: A Self-worth Perspective on Motivation and School Reform*, Cambridge: Cambridge University Press.

Csikszentmihalyi, M. (1990) *Flow: The Psychology of Optimal Experience*, New York: Harper and Row.

De Charms, R. (1968) *Personal Causation: The Internal Affective Determinants of Behaviour*, New York: Academic Press.

De Charms, R. (1976) *Enhancing Motivation: Change in the Classroom*, New York: Irvington.

Deci, E. L. (1975) *Intrinsic Motivation*, New York: Plenum.

Deci, E. L., Koestner, R., and Ryan, R. M. (1999) 'A Meta-analytic Review of Experiments Examining the Effects of Extrinsic Rewards on Intrinsic Motivation', 125 *Psychological Bulletin*, pp. 627–668.

Deci, E. L. and Moller, A. C. (2005) 'The Concept of Competence: A Starting Place for Understanding Intrinsic Motivation and Self-determined Extrinsic motivation', in Elliot, A. J. and Dweck, C. S. (eds), *Handbook of Competence and Motivation*, New York: Guilford Press.

Department for Education and Skills (2000) *Working with Teaching Assistants: A Good Practice Guide*, London: DfES Publications.

Department for Education and Skills (2001) *Special Educational Needs Code of Practice*, London: DfES Publications.

Department for Education and Skills (2003) *Raising Standards and Tackling Workload: A National Agreement*, London: DfES Publications.

Department for Education and Skills (2004a) *Teaching Assistant File: Induction Training for Teaching Assistants*, DfES 0585/2004 (Primary), London: DfES Publications.

Department for Education and Skills (2004b) *Teaching Assistant File: Induction Training for Teaching Assistants*, DfES 0586/2004 (Secondary) London: DfES Publications.

Department for Education and Skills (2004c) *Removing Barriers to Achievement: The Government's Strategy for SEN*, London: DfES Publications.

Devecchi, C. (2005) 'Teachers and TAs Working Together in a Secondary School: Should We Be Critical?' paper presented at BERA Conference, University of Glamorgan, 14–17 September.

Devecchi, C. and Rouse, M. (2010) 'An Exploration of the Features of Effective Collaboration between Teachers and Teaching Assistants in Secondary Schools', 25(2) *Support for Learning*, pp. 91–99.

Dixon, A. (2003) 'Teaching Assistants: Whose Definition?', 45(1) *Forum*, pp. 26–29.

Dornyei, Z. (2001) *Teaching and Researching Motivation*, London: Pearson Education Limited.

Dweck, C. S. (1975) 'The Role of Expectations and Attributions in the Alleviation of Learned Helplessness', 31 *Journal of Personality and Social Psychology*, pp. 674–685.

Dweck, C. S. (2000) *Self-Theories: Their Role in Motivation, Personality and Development*, Hove: Psychology Press.

Dweck, C.S. (2008a) 'Brainology Transforming Students' Motivation to Learn', 67(2) *Independent School*, pp. 110–119.

Dweck, C.S. (2008b) *Mindset: The New Psychology of Success*, New York: Ballantine Books.

Dweck, C. S. and Leggett, E. L. (1988) A Social-Cognitive Approach to Motivation and Personality, 95 *Psychological Review*, pp. 256–273.

Eccles, J. S. and Wigfield, A. (1995) 'In the Mind of the Actor: The Structures of Adolescents' Achievement Task Values and Expectancy-related Beliefs, 21 *Personality and Social Psychology Bulletin*, pp. 215–25.

Eccles, J. S., Wigfield, A. and Schiefele, A. (1998) 'Motivation to Succeed', in Damon, W. and Eisenberg, N. (eds) *Handbook of Child Psychology Volume 3: Social, Emotional and Personality Development* (5th Edition), New York: John Wiley and Sons.

Edmond, N. (2003) 'School-based Learning: Constraints and Limitations in Learning from School Experience for Teaching Assistants', 29(2) *Journal of Education for Teaching*, pp. 113–123

Elliot, N. (2010) 'Building Consensus: Negotiating, Listening, Influencing and Sustaining Communication: Learning from Danny', in Hallet, F. and Hallet, G. (eds), *Transforming the Role of the SENCO: Achieving the National Award for SEN Coordination*, Maidenhead: Open University Press.

Elwood, J. (2006) 'Formative Assessment: Possibilities, Boundaries and Limitations', 13(2) *Assessment in Education: Principles, Policy and Practice*, pp. 215–232.

Fox, G. (2003) *A Handbook for Learning Support Assistants: Teachers and Assistants Working Together* (9th revised edition), London: David Fulton Publishers.

Freeman, J. (1998) *Educating the Very Able*, London: TSO/Ofsted.

Galloway, D., Rogers, C., Armstrong, D. and Leo, E. (1998) *Motivating the Difficult to Teach*, London and New York: Longman.

Gardner, H. (1993) *Frames of Mind: The Theory of Multiple Intelligences*, New York: Basic Books.

Gardner, H. (2006) *Multiple Intelligences: New Horizons in Theory and Practice*, New York: Basic Books.

Gilbert, I. (2002) *Essential Motivation in the Classroom*, London: Routledge Falmer.

Gottfried, A. E. (1990) 'Academic Intrinsic Motivation in Young Elementary School Children', 82 *Journal of Educational Psychology*, pp. 525–538.

Graham, S. (1994) 'Classroom Motivation from an Attributional Perspective', in O'Neil, Jr., H. F. and Drillings, M. (eds) *Motivation Theory and Research*, Hillsdale, NJ: Lawrence Erlbaum.

Grotberg, E. H. (1995) *A Guide to Promoting Resilience in Children: Strengthening the Human Spirit*, available online http://resilnet.uiuc.edu/library/grotb95b.html (accessed 4th November 2011).

Hammersley-Fletcher, L. and Lowe, M. (2005) 'Remodelling Schools: Experiences from Within "Change Teams"', paper presented at BERA Conference, University of Glamorgan, 14–17 September.

Hargreaves, D. H. (1967) *Social Relations in a Secondary School*, London: Routledge and Kegan Paul.

Hargreaves, D. H. (1982) *The Challenge for the Comprehensive School: Culture, Curriculum and Community*, London: Routledge and Kegan Paul.

Harlen, W. (2006) 'The Role of Assessment in Developing Motivation for Learning', in Gardner, J. (ed.), *Assessment and Learning*, London: Sage.

Harlen, W. and Deakin-Crick, R. (2002) *Testing, Motivation and Learning*, Cambridge: University of Cambridge Faculty of Education.

Harlen, W. and Deakin-Crick, R. (2003) 'Testing and Motivation for Learning', 10(2) *Assessment in Education: Principles, Policy and Practice*, pp. 169–207.

Harter, S. (1978) 'Effectance Motivation Reconsidered: Toward a Developmental Model', 21 *Human Development*, pp. 34–64.

Harter, S. (1982) 'The Perceived Competence Scale for Children', 53 *Child Development*, pp. 87–97.

Harter, S. (1996) 'Teacher and Classmate Influences on Scholastic Motivation, Self-esteem and Level of Voice in Adolescents', in Juvonen, J. and Wentzel, K. R. (eds), *Social Motivation: Understanding Children's School Adjustment*, Cambridge: Cambridge University Press.

Harter, S. and Connell, J.P. (1984) 'A Comparison of Children's Achievement and Related Self-perceptions of Competence, Control and Motivational Orientation', in Nicholls, J. G. (ed.) *Advances in Motivation and Achievement: The Development of Achievement Motivation, Vol. 3*, Greenwich, CT: JAI Press.

Heckhausen, H. (1991) *Motivation and Action*, Berlin: Springer-Verlag.

Hull, C. L. (1943) *Principles of Behavior*, New York: Appleton-Century-Crofts.

Hutchins, R. (2010) *An Ethnographic Investigation into Children's Perceptions of Assessment for Learning*, unpublished Institution-Focused Study, Institute of Education, University of London.

Kuhl, J. (1984) 'Volitional Aspects of Achievement Motivation and Learned Helplessnes: Toward a Comprehensive Theory of Action Control', in Maher, B. A. (ed.), *Progress in Experimental Personality Research, Vol. 13*, New York: Academic Press.

Lacey, P. (1999) *On a Wing and a Prayer*, London: Mencap.

Lee, L. (1999), 'Teachers' Conceptions of Gifted and Talented Young Children', 10(2) *High Ability Studies*, pp. 183–196.

Lepper, M. R., Corpus, J. H., and Iyengar, S. S. (2005) 'Intrinsic and Extrinsic Motivational Orientations in the Classroom: Age Differences and Academic Correlates', 97 *Journal of Educational Psychology*, pp. 184–196.

Lepper, M. R. and Greene, D. (1978) 'Over-justification Research and Beyond: Toward a Means-end Analysis of Intrinsic and Extrinsic Motivation', in Lepper, M. R. and Greene, D. (eds.), *The Hidden Costs of Reward: New Perspectives on the Psychology of Human Motivation*, Hillsdale, NJ: Erlbaum.

Lepper, M. R. and Henderlong, J. (2000) 'Turning "Play" into "Work" and "Work" into "Play": 25 years of Research on Intrinsic versus Extrinsic Motivation', in Sansone, C. and Harachiewicz, J. (eds), *Intrinsic and Extrinsic Motivation: The Search for Optimal Motivation and Performance*, San Diego, CA: Academic Press.

Locke, E. A. (1996) 'Motivation through Conscious Goal Setting', 5 *Applied and Preventative Psychology*, pp. 117–124.

Locke, E. A. and Latham, G. P. (1990) *A Theory of Goal Setting and Task Performance*, Englewood Cliffs, NJ: Prentice Hall.

Lorenz, S. (1998) *Effective In-class Support: The Management of Support Staff in Mainstream and Special Schools*, London: David Fulton Publishers.

Maehr, M. L. and Midgley, C. (1991) 'Enhancing Student Motivation: A Schoolwide Approach', 26 *Educational Psychologist*, pp. 399–427.

Marsh, P., Rosser, E. and Harre, R. (1978) *The Rules of Disorder*, London: Routledge.

Marshall, B. and Drummond, M. (2006), 'How Teachers Engage with Assessment for Learning: Lessons from the Classroom', 21(2) *Research Papers in Education*, pp. 133–149.

Marshall, B. and Wiliam, D. (2006) *English Inside the Black Box*, Chiswick: NferNelson.

Marton, F. and Booth, S. (1997) *Learning and Awareness*, Mahwah, NJ: Lawrence Erlbaum Associates.

Masten, A. S. (2001) Ordinary Magic: Resilience Processes in Development, 56 *American Psychologist*, pp. 227–238.

McLean, A. (2009) *Motivating Every Learner*, London: Sage.

McNamara, E. (1999) *Positive Pupil Management and Motivation*, London: David Fulton Publishers.

McNamara, E. (2009) (ed.) *Motivational Interviewing: Theory, Practice and Applications with Children and Young People*, Ainsdale, Merseyside: Positive Behaviour Management.

Mead, G.H. (1934) *Mind, Self and Society*, Chicago: University of Chicago Press.

Mertler, C. (2009), 'Teachers' Assessment Knowledge and their Perceptions of the Impact of Classroom Assessment Professional Development', 12(2) *Improving Schools*, pp. 101–113.

Midgley, C., Kaplan, A., Middleton, M., Maehr, M., Urdan, T., Hicks Anderman, L., Anderman, E., and Roeser, R. (1998) 'The Development and Validation of Scales Assessing Students' Achievement Goal Orientations', 23 *Educational Psychology*, pp. 113–131.

Moni, K., van Kraayenoord, C. and Baker, C. (2002) 'Students' Perceptions of Literacy Assessment', 9(3) *Assessment in Education: Principles, Policy and Practice*, pp. 319–342.

Muijs, D. (2003) 'The Effectiveness in the Use of Learning Support Assistants in Improving the Mathematics Achievement of Low Achieving Pupils in a Primary School', 45(3) *Educational Research*, pp. 219–230.

Nicholls, J.G. (1990) 'What is Ability and Why are we Mindful of it? A Developmental Perspective', in Sternberg, R., and Kolligian, J. (eds.), *Competence Considered*, New Haven, CT: Yale University Press.

Perrenoud, P. (1998) 'From Formative Evaluation to a Controlled Regulation of Learning Processes: Towards a Wider Conceptual Field', 5(1) *Assessment in Education: Principles, Policy and Practice*, pp. 85–102.

Persson, R. (1998) 'Paragons of Virtue: Teachers' Conceptual Understanding of High Ability in an Egalitarian School System', 9(2) *High Ability Studies*, pp. 181–196.

Phillips, N. and Lindsay, G. (2006) 'Motivation in Gifted Students', 17(1) *High Ability Studies*, pp. 57–73.

Prochaska, J. O. and DiClemente, C. C. (1982) *The Transtheoretical Approach: Crossing Traditional Boundaries of Therapy*, Homewood, IL: Dowe Jones/Irwin.

Quicke, J. (2003) 'Teaching Assistants: Students or Servants?' 45(2) *Forum*, pp. 71–74.

Radford, M. (2006) 'Researching Classrooms: Complexity and Chaos', 32(2) *British Educational Research Journal*, pp. 177–190.

Relich, J. D., Debus, R. and Walker, R. (1986) 'The Mediating Role of Attribution and Self-efficacy Variables for Treatment Effects on Achievement Outcomes', 11 *Contemporary Educational Psychology*, pp. 195–216.

Rose, R. (2000) 'Using Classroom Support in a Primary School', 27 *British Journal of Special Education*, pp. 191–196.

Rosenthal, R. and Jacobson, L. (1966) 'Teachers' Expectancies: Determinants of Pupils' IQ Gains', 19 *Psychological Reports*, pp. 115–118.

Ryan, R. M. and Deci, E. L. (2000) 'Intrinsic and Extrinsic Motivations: Classic Definitions and New Directions', 25 *Contemporary Educational Psychology*, pp. 54–67.

Sadler, D. (1989) 'Formative Assessment and the Design of Instructional Systems', 18 *Instructional Science*, pp. 119–144.

Sadler, D. (1998) 'Formative Assessment: Revisiting the Territory', 5(1) *Assessment in Education: Principles, Policy and Practice*, pp. 77–84.

Schraw, G. and Lehman S. (2001) 'Situational Interest: A Review of the Literature and Directions for Future Research', 13 *Educational Psychology Review*, pp. 23–52.

Schunk, D. H., Pintrich, P. R., and Meece, J. L. (2010) *Motivation in Education: Theory, Research and Applications* (3rd edition), Upper Saddle River, NJ: Pearson Education International.

Scott, D. (2011) 'Global or Subject-Specific? How do Children Attribute and What is the Effect of an Attributional Retraining Programme?', unpublished MA (Education) dissertation, University of Chichester.

Smith, C., Dakers, J., Dow, W., Head, G., Sutherland, M. and Irwin, R. (2005) *A Systematic Review of What Pupils, Aged 11–16, Believe Impacts on their Motivation to Learn in the Classroom*, London: EPPI-Centre, Social Science Research Unit, Institute of Education, University of London.

Smith, L. (2010) 'Revealing the Riches? Pupil Voice in the Foundation Stage: A Case Study', unpublished MA (Education) dissertation, University of Chichester

Spirito, A., Stark, L. J., and Williams, C. (1988) 'Development of a Brief Checklist to Assess Coping in Pediatric Patients', 13 *Journal of Pediatric Psychology*, pp. 555–574.

Sternberg, R. (2001) 'Giftedness as Developing Expertise: A Theory of the Interface between High Abilities and Achieved Excellence', 12(2) *High Ability Studies*, pp. 159–179.

Sykes, J. B. (ed.) (1986) *The Concise Oxford Dictionary*, Oxford: Clarendon Press.

Torrance, H. (2007) 'Assessment as Learning? How the Use of Explicit Learning Objectives, Assessment Criteria and Feedback in Post-secondary Education and Training Can Come to Dominate Learning', 13(3) *Assessment in Education: Principles, Policy and Practice,* pp. 281–294.

Tripp, D. (1993) *Critical Incidents in Teaching: Developing Professional Judgement*, London: Routledge.

Urdan, T. and Maehr, M. (1995) 'Beyond a Two Goal Theory of Motivation: A Case for Social Goals', 65 *Review of Educational Research*, pp. 213–244.

Urdan, T. and Turner, J. C. (2005) 'Competence Motivation in the Classroom', in Elliot, A. J. and Dweck, C. S. (eds), *Handbook of Competence and Motivation*, New York, Guilford Press.

Vygotsky, L. (1978) *Mind in Society*, London: Harvard University Press.

Vygotsky, L. (1986) *Thought and Language*, Cambridge, MA: The MIT Press.

Watkinson, A. (2003) *Managing Teaching Assistants: A Guide for Headteachers, Managers and Teachers*, London: Routledge Falmer.

Webb, M. E. and Jones, J. (2009) 'Exploring Tensions in Developing Assessment for Learning', 16(2) *Assessment in Education: Principles, Policy and Practice*, pp. 165–184.

Weiner, B. (1986) *An Attributional Theory of Motivation and Emotion*, New York: Springer-Verlag.

Weiner, B. (1992) *Human Motivation, Metaphors, Theories and Research*, Newbury Park, CA: Sage.

Wenger, E. (1998) *Communities of Practice*, Cambridge: Cambridge University Press.

Wiliam, D. (2009) *Assessment for Learning: Why, What and How?* London: Institute of Education, University of London.

Youell, B. (2006) *The Learning Relationship: Psychoanalytic Thinking in Education*, London: Karnac.

Zimmerman, B. J. (2000) 'Attaining Self-regulation: A Social Cognitive Perspective', in Boekaerts, M., Pintrich, P. R., and Aeidner, M. (eds), *Handbook of Self-Regulation*, San Diego: Academic Press.

Index